'Le Corbusier, this theorist,
this artist, who to my mind
can never be sufficiently
praised nor sufficiently
condemned . . .'
Pierre Francastel

'Houses are built to live in
and not to look on: therefore,
let use be preferred before
Uniformity, except where
both may be had . . .'
Francis Bacon

Philippe Boudon

Lived-in Architecture

Le Corbusier's
Pessac revisited

Translated by Gerald Onn

With a preface by
Henri Lefèbvre,
Professor in the Faculté
des Lettres et
Sciences humaines at
Nanterre University

The MIT Press,
Cambridge, Massachusetts

First English language edition 1972
ISBN 262 02 0831
Library of Congress Catalog No. 70–155321

Designed by Herbert Spencer
Made and printed in Great Britain by
Lund Humphries, Bradford and London

CONTENTS

Preface

Although at first sight this 'case study' may seem light and insubstantial, in actual fact it is pregnant with meaning. Some forty years ago, at Pessac near Bordeaux, the most celebrated architect and town planner of modern times, a man who contributed at both a practical and a theoretical level to urban development, built a new settlement – the Quartiers Modernes Frugès. What was Le Corbusier trying to do at Pessac? By building in a modern style and by taking due account of economic and social problems he hoped to produce low-cost houses that would be pleasant to live in; he wanted to provide people with a container, in which they could install themselves and live their daily lives; in his dual capacity as architect and town planner he wanted to create a functional system based on technological criteria; and to this end he set out to design predetermined, homogeneous and essentially cubist structures, in which open and closed areas would complement one another.

This was what Le Corbusier wanted. But what did he actually achieve? Perhaps it was because he was a genius and because (for better or worse) men of genius never do precisely what they set out to do, but the fact of the matter is that in Pessac Le Corbusier produced a kind of architecture that lent itself to conversion and sculptural ornamentation. And what did the occupants do? Instead of installing themselves in their containers, instead of adapting to them and living in them 'passively', they decided that as far as possible they were going to live 'actively'. In doing so they showed what living in a house really is: an activity. They took what had been offered to them and worked on it, converted it, added to it. What did they add? Their needs. They created distinctions, whose significance is analysed in this book. They introduced personal qualities. They built a differentiated social cluster.

Philippe Boudon's subtle analysis of the distinctions, of the 'topical' qualities, introduced, or rather *produced*, by the Pessac occupants in what was originally an undifferentiated urban setting has helped to further urban studies. It may well be that he has carried them further even than he realizes, for he has drawn attention to different *levels* of reality and different *levels* of thought. In his enquiry he illustrates, or perhaps I should say demonstrates, the existence of three distinct levels.

(a) First there is the *theoretical level*, at which theory tends to merge with ideology or, to be more precise, is not usually sufficiently distinguished from ideology. This is the level at which our architects and town planners operate. They deal with empirical problems by reference to town-planning ideologies. And they do so with or without the approval of the public institutions and political organizations, but always at their level, a procedure that is not without its risks. These ideological dangers are discussed by Philippe Boudon in the light of Le Corbusier's experiment and the 'social requirements' formulated by Henry Frugès for the Pessac project.

(b) Then there is the *practical level*, at which ideological considerations are supplemented by other, quite different factors. Here the architect exercises his mind and his will, bringing them to bear on the practical needs of the future occupants. Some of these needs are clearly recognized, others are not. And so Le Corbusier's architectural practice is seen to be more hesitant, more flexible and more vital than his architectural theory. But both ideological and theoretical considerations are forced to give way in the face of reality.

(c) Finally, there is the *town-planning level*, at which a certain way of life, a certain style (or absence of style) makes itself felt. The social activities of individual occupants and groups of occupants, which have been influenced to a greater or lesser degree by the different groupings within the district, are seen for what they are. At this level we find a specific topology, a concrete rationality that is more impressive and more complex than abstract rationality.

In his study Philippe Boudon analyses the relationship between architecture and town planning and also considers the *practical ramifications* of urban design (a form of enquiry which is almost completely new and which has virtually been inaugurated by him). He introduces material that casts a new light on the problems posed by town planning and will help us to form a general assessment covering all aspects of this discipline, which is the only profitable way of tackling and perhaps solving these problems.

Henri Lefèbvre

Introduction

'If you cross the Landes by rail you will find yourself completely capti-
vated, a few minutes out of Bordeaux, by the sight of a strange village.
About a hundred houses with sober, massive and rectilinear forms,
painted brown, white or pale green, arrest the traveller's attention and
excite his curiosity. But the train passes quickly ... I was so impressed
by this unexpected view that the next day, when I was returning by the
same route, I stopped off at Bordeaux to visit this unusual settlement,
whose architecture proved to be every bit as novel and bold as I had
imagined. There I was able to observe a new style, a completely new
and, in my opinion, successful conception of what a modern house
ought to be: a "machine to live in" ...'

That is how the 'Quartiers Modernes Frugès', which were built in
Pessac by Le Corbusier, appeared to a journalist on the staff of the
magazine *Mon chez moi* in 1926.

After forty years, of course, one would expect the district to look
different, but that it could have changed so much appears quite incred-
ible. It seems that everybody has now converted his 'machine to live in'
into a 'chez soi' ... Not only have the colours disappeared in the vast
majority of cases but the 'wide windows' have been made narrower, the
patios have been enclosed, many of the original terraces have been
roofed over, the empty spaces beneath the stilts have been blocked off,
and the great crop of sheds that has sprung up, much to the detriment
of the architecture, helps to create a general impression of dilapidation.
This impression is sufficiently pronounced for the visitor to feel that, in
addition to the normal processes of ageing, there has also been a real

1

conflict between what the architect intended and what the occupants wanted.

In this conflict the architect considered himself to be in the wrong: 'You know, it is always life that is right and the architect who is wrong . . .', Le Corbusier once said when speaking of Pessac. And, in point of fact, one's initial reaction is to conclude that this project actually was an architectural failure. But to speak of failure in this sense would be to assume that architecture is immutable and that architects are capable of satisfying their clients' deepest habitational needs. In fact, the mere definition of these needs, which are still obscure, would presuppose that they were capable of existing independently of any living context, which is hardly likely. However, it seemed that, far from isolating illusory general truths, a study in depth – carried out within a clearly defined and limited context – of the motivations which had persuaded the residents of Pessac to convert their houses to such an extent would be able to cast light on specific aspects of 'living' and clarify the relationship between the architect's original conception and the residents' reactions. And so we carried out an enquiry at Pessac in which we recorded any alterations that had been made to the buildings and also interviewed many of the occupants.

In instituting this enquiry I was not trying to prove any particular thesis but rather to draw attention to the problems involved, open up new paths of investigation, clarify a number of new conceptions and – since enquiries of this kind are still something of a rarity – to test rather than employ a method. There was no certainty, when I embarked on my enquiry, that I would obtain a definite result. And, in fact, it turned out – as I had expected – that no peremptory conclusions could be drawn. But I had the definite impression that the 'Quartiers Modernes Frugès' – or the Q.M.F. as I shall frequently be calling them in the chapters that follow – were an architectural and social experiment that had developed naturally and freely and was likely to prove a fertile source of ideas. Although it is not possible to draw any direct analogies (fortunately living is far too complex a phenomenon for it to be reduced to a system of simple co-ordinates) and although it is unlikely that we shall ever possess a precise formula for living (a neat list of human needs that could be catered for in our homes), it remains none the less true that both the way in which we live and the homes we live in are products of the human mind and as such are subject to constant modification. From this it follows that they cannot be defined in terms of past achievements. But they can be illuminated by experiment, and it is the lessons learned from the Pessac experiment that I have tried to convey.

M. Frugès, the industrialist who provided the financial backing for the project, insisted that the whole new district should be regarded as *a laboratory*, in which Le Corbusier would be able to 'put his

2

theories into practice and carry them to their most extreme conclusions'.

Since laboratories exist not merely for putting theories into practice – although only too frequently this constitutes the full extent of architectural activity in this sphere – but also for testing those theories under controlled conditions, it seemed to me that the Q.M.F. offered a unique opportunity of pursuing an enquiry into the ecology of dwellings, which would place the work of one of our greatest modern architects in juxtaposition to the suburban style of architecture apparently favoured by the majority of the occupants who made modifications to their homes.

The need to study the problem from a sociological as well as an architectural point of view prompted me to seek the help of sociologists:[1] although it was very tempting for me, as an architect, to rush in with my own explanation of what had happened at Pessac, the temptation had to be resisted; for I was primarily interested in discovering what the occupants thought about it, and it would have been a pity to have projected my own *architectural* ideas into a study which was being carried out for the express purpose of illuminating the disparity of view between the architect and the householders. On the other hand, I felt that the study should be conducted by an architect since he would be better equipped to describe and demonstrate the various problems of spatial organization. Above all, it was imperative that the person who interpreted the alterations should be able to 'read' them correctly. This called for a basic knowledge of the kind of problems posed by spatial, structural and – in a general way – architectural requirements, with which only architects are accustomed to deal, the general public tending to be unversed in such matters. I also felt that, by adopting this procedure, I would be able to correlate the different material that I would be receiving, thus presenting a collective interpretation.

Finally, it should be pointed out that this study is not concerned solely with Le Corbusier. True, his personality and his architecture are by no means unappreciable factors and, in fact, constitute one important aspect of the problem, the other consisting of the occupants' reactions to his architecture. In this particular case the architecture was anything but impersonal; as for the residents of Pessac, they are quite distinct from the residents of any other region or country. But, although this study is essentially local and circumscribed, I hope that it will none the less help to throw light on the more general phenomenon of the conflict between the original intentions of the architect, as expressed in his buildings, and the reactions of the people who live in them.

As far as Pessac is concerned, we shall act on the assumption that such a conflict has taken place.

[1] I wish to thank Raymond and Monique Fichelet, who organized the group discussion and also obtained the valuable services of Claude Nedelec, who collaborated on the interviews.

In addition to the interpretations which I have advanced, the material presented in this book may very well suggest other interpretations to the reader. As I have already pointed out, my principal object has been to report a particular experiment, in which habitational, architectural and urban factors interacted on a small and intimate scale. Consequently, where I have felt that the verbatim reproduction of original material might prove of interest to the reader I have not hesitated to adopt this course. On many occasions it has seemed to me that press articles, printed texts and interviews have spoken for themselves; in such cases I have preferred to let them do so.

PART ONE

'It was in vain that I asked him to put himself in the place of the prospective purchasers, whose eyes are accustomed to decorative effects, even though they may be of the most discreet kind . . .'
Henry Frugès

1
Historical account of the project

The Pessac project was undertaken as a direct result of the small group of ten houses which Le Corbusier built for M. Frugès at Lège, near the dockyards of Arcachon, in 1920.[1] Henry Frugès's father owned a factory nearby which produced packing cases for the sugar industry. But every year, during the pine resin harvest, the sawmill suffered from absenteeism. In order to resolve his labour problem the industrialist conceived the idea of building houses for his workmen and asked Henry Frugès, who had acquired some knowledge of architecture from his two architect uncles, to carry out a project for ten houses. Frugès started on the project when he read an article by 'an unknown architect', Le Corbusier, in a journal entitled *L'Esprit Nouveau*. He was completely carried away by the ideas that he found there, and he explained his infatuation in the following passage:

'What did he [Le Corbusier] advocate?
'After the 1914–1918 war and the destruction of countless houses in France it was a matter of urgency to build new houses in order to give millions of people

[1] The houses in Lège, which were conceived along very similar lines to those in Pessac, have suffered from a form of rural mimesis that is even more disfiguring than the suburban mimesis found in Pessac. Today it is difficult to perceive in these imitation farmhouses any trace of Le Corbusier's original design, which was far ahead of its time and consequently remained unrecognized. The only things that give any hint of the original condition of these houses are the narrow metal fittings.

a roof over their head. Why, Le Corbusier asked, should we not make use of the method developed towards the end of the war, which had made it possible to construct kilometres of trench in record time? For we could then build wide windows like the windows in the corridors of railway coaches and replace tiled roofs by terraces . . . He also advanced several other highly ingenious ideas, including one very clever scheme for conducting rainwater through the interior of the house so as to avoid damage to outside pipes during thaws . . .'

After reading this article Frugès wrote immediately to Le Corbusier and asked him to design the ten houses for Lège. But in July 1967 Henry Frugès, the instigator and promoter of this project, told his own story to the residents of Pessac at a fête organized by the town council to celebrate the fortieth anniversary of the Q.M.F. So let him speak for himself:

'I had told him: "do it in your own way", and a year later, in 1921, the ten villas were completed and occupied.
'An embryonic form of town planning. I had included in the plan a wall for *pelote basque*, gardens around each villa, a public square, etc. . . . Flowers everywhere, including the terraces . . . central heating run from a kitchen boiler, which I had installed on my own account. Drainage for toilets and waste water by septic tank, and various other modern amenities.
'Since I possessed the necessary machines – which, incidentally, were extremely expensive (cement gun, compressor, ball mills and mixers purchased from the Ingersoll-Rand company) – and wanted to make my contribution to the national task of helping the homeless, I decided to build a garden city on a larger scale, comprising about one hundred and fifty to two hundred villas. I chose Pessac, which was famous for the pure air of its pine trees, as the site for this settlement. I acquired an extensive area of meadowland surrounded by a pine forest, and we worked out a general plan. We then realized that, if we wanted to leave adequate spaces between the villas, we would have to reduce the total number of buildings and settled on one hundred as a maximum. But after the fifty-first house had been built fate intervened and brought my project to a halt.
'Before considering the layout of the villas and their gardens we returned to Lège and asked the ten house-

holders there to tell us quite frankly about any defects or inconveniences they had discovered; and their observations enabled us to improve on certain arrangements in our new designs.

'For a while we were divided by a difference of opinion as to the kind of houses that ought to be built. Le Corbusier had already started to think *on a grand scale*[2] and was dreaming of skyscrapers. I myself wanted to offer the future owners individual family houses. In the end we agreed that some of the villas should be individual dwellings whilst others should be designed for two families. Garages standard. Wide windows. Terraces constructed to take a layer of earth sixty centimetres deep so that plants, such as rosebushes, would have an ample depth of soil. Internal rain water pipes. Central heating run from a kitchen boiler which, like the hot and cold water systems, I provided as a standard fitting. Electricity. Showerbath with a direct temperature control of my own invention. Septic tank.

'I had fruit trees and ornamental shrubs planted in every garden and trees on all the public roads.

'A further difference of opinion between Le Corbusier and myself: with his inveterate hatred of all forms of decoration (which stemmed from his Protestant background and the general austerity of his personality) he wanted to leave the walls completely unfinished so that they still showed the marks of the shuttering. I was flabbergasted. He told me that, if we wished to offer the houses to the public at the lowest possible price, we could not afford to spend money on unnecessary luxuries. He then launched into a diatribe against ornamentation, exclaiming: "we are tired of décor, what we need is a good visual laxative! Bare walls, total simplicity, that is how to restore our visual sense!"

'. . . I understood him only too well, because we both wanted to build economically, but he did not understand me! It was in vain that I asked him to put himself in the place of the future purchasers, whose eyes are accustomed to decorative effects, even though they may be of the most discreet kind. Those purchasers will take fright and walk out on us, I wrote to him. It is absolutely essential that we should attract their attention *agreeably* and, if we

---

[2] The italics in this extract are H. Frugès's.

are to do so, then – apart from the interior amenities, which they will not be able to appreciate until they live in their villas – we must show them some pleasing element on the exterior. The first thing we have to do is persuade them to live there. Consequently, there must be *something about the exterior that pleases them.*

'At that moment the Muse of Painting – whom I had christened Chromyris at one of my conferences on the subject of "Art and Beauty" came to my aid. She gave me the idea of painting the façades of the villas in different colours, properly thought out and carefully chosen so that they would harmonize with one another and also be visible, depending on the distance, from the other side of the green areas. My tenacity found a powerful ally in my adversary: he too was a painter with a penchant for colour harmonies; and so, thanks to Chromyris, we reached agreement. We then studied different colours and their values and made the following selection: horizon blue (the colour of our soldiers' uniforms at the end of the war), golden yellow, jade green, off white and maroon, the maroon being a subtle mixture of red ochre and brown. Each façade was painted in one of these colours. By the time it was all finished, it was an enchanting sight; the colours of the walls on the different villas harmonized quite marvellously with the brightly coloured flowers and the green vegetation in the gardens and also with one another.

'An error of judgement on my part then held us up for a whole year; thinking to provide work for the people of the district I turned to a local builder. The result was a catastrophe. But then, thanks to M. Vrinat, an engineer employed in our factories whom I had seconded to supervise the work at Pessac, we were able to proceed on a proper basis with the help of a prominent builder from Paris, M. Summer, whom Le Corbusier had persuaded to join us. Shortly afterwards, more than two hundred workers were on the site and progress was made at the rate of two villas (main structures) per week.

'My friend together with his young cousin Pierre Jeanneret drew up the plan. Originally, I had expressed a desire for *the greatest possible variety in the designs,* which would have meant that, ideally, no two villas would have been exactly the same. But I was soon persuaded by my friend that this view was exaggerated.

It was then decided that some of the houses would be identical in form and appearance and would be arranged in small groups; others would be linked by a continuous façade whilst yet others would be set out in complete isolation in their own grounds.

'Moreover, the diversity which I wished to achieve had to be reconciled with the need for serial production, since this was the only way of reducing costs to any appreciable extent.

'Le Corbusier's solution to this problem was derived from the principles underlying the games of "patience" and "lotto": since various fixtures could be joined together or separated as desired by the householder he adopted a module of 5 metres by 5 metres, a demi-module of 5 metres by 2·5 metres and a quarter module of 2·5 metres by 2·5 metres. By playing around with these three elements, by placing them in different alignments, it was possible to obtain considerable diversity without forgoing the advantages of serial production. Finally – within this same context of "multiplicity in unity", which is one of the immutable principles of Art and one of the laws of Beauty – curved forms were specified instead of rectilinear forms.

'On June 13, 1926, M. de Monzie, the Minister of Public Works, accompanied by numerous important persons from Paris, came to open the *Quartiers Modernes Frugès*. The ceremony was also attended by the leading citizens of Bordeaux and Aquitaine, whom I had invited to be present. An immense crowd invaded the site. "Site" is the right word, for at that time the majority of the villas were still under construction. In fact, only five had been completed, two of which were fully furnished. I had contacted the director of the "Dames de France", who had arranged everything so well that the two villas really gave the impression of being lived in. It was on the terrace of villa No.44, which stood in its own grounds, that I received the Minister. I explained to him what we had been trying to achieve, after which Le Corbusier provided more detailed information for the benefit of the ministerial aides.

'It is difficult to assess the balance of forces on that memorable and historic occasion. But, judging by the reactions that I heard and the soundings that I was able to make, I do not think that the following table of public reactions is all that far removed from the truth:

Enthusiastic   1%
Sympathetic   2%
Hesitant   2%
Worried and stupefied   40%
Convinced that I had gone mad   55%

'It was probably those in the last category who coined the sobriquet *Rigolarium* to describe this complex of novel structures; for in France, as everyone knows, everything is ultimately a *rigolade* . . .'[3]

Does this passage give an adequate impression of Henry Frugès? The promoter of the Pessac project, a man of enormous vitality, once described himself as 'a seeker, multivalent artist, architect (without a diploma), painter (working in every genre from fresco to miniatures on ivory grounds), sculptor, pianist and composer, member of the S.A.C.E.M.[4] of Paris, author, art critic, historian and so on . . .'

In a letter which he wrote to me about the Pessac project he said: 'My fellow townsmen were particularly disturbed by these new and extremely simple forms because they were, and still are, imbued with the stylistic features of seventeenth- and eighteenth-century architecture, which produced some splendid monuments and private residences in Bordeaux.
'Although I am myself a great admirer of such architecture, when I built my own residence in Bordeaux between 1913 and 1924, I did not set out to reproduce a seventeenth-century building but tried instead to create a sort of museum of modern art. This building, which was intended as an act of homage to my native town, was inspired by Gothic art which, in my opinion, produced the most perfect of all architectural styles; the most beautiful of the Gothic cathedrals I consider superior even to the Parthenon and the Angkor-Vat! Do I shock you? . . .
'Since I am also a great admirer of Mohammedan art forms I tried to amalgamate the Gothic with a particular

[3] rigolade = a joke.
[4] Société des Auteurs Compositeurs et Editeurs de Musique.

kind of Mohammedan style, not by making an arbitrary
"assortment" of different purely material elements but
by achieving a chemical "combination", for in these two
styles there are several features that are very closely
related. Needless to say, I also added my own ideas.'

Today, at 85 years of age, Frugès is still carrying on with his hectic
artistic pursuits: at present he is completing an 'heraldic dictionary',
written, illustrated and bound by hand, and is also engaged on a transla-
tion of Arabian novels, which will appear in a handwritten edition with
illuminated illustrations painted in egg tempera which he mixes himself.
Other works in progress include an opera and a comedy. The walls of
his house are covered with his pictures. 'After spending two years at
the H.E.C.[5] I am still not a business man', he once observed.

And, in point of fact, in 1929 – by which time his father had died –
Frugès faced financial ruin and became subject to depressive states.
Acting on medical advice he went to recuperate in Algeria. It was not
until he returned to France, some forty years later, that he saw the
completed project at Pessac.

What sort of man is Henry Frugès?

'A natural phenomenon', according to Le Corbusier.

'A true artist', according to the residents of Pessac, who like and
admire him – a just reward for his paternalism:

> M 1 — For my part,[6] I think that what they should copy, above
> all . . . above all, it's Frugès they should copy . . . Le
> Corbusier, of course, he had ideas . . . progressive ideas
> . . . But nobody ever says very much about Frugès's ideas.
> And, you know, it's a sad thing, but there haven't been
> very many people at any time who've thought on such a
> scale . . . I'm talking about Frugès. Do you honestly
> think that today there would be many patrons who would
> *even consider* such a project! . . . And, you know, it
> ruined him . . . You've seen Frugès . . . well, damnation,
> man . . . damnation! . . .

Frugès's assessment of local reaction to his project would appear to have
been reasonably accurate. M. Vrinat, the engineer responsible for the
construction work, told us that they were constantly running into
difficulties over building permits and authorizations for different
processes, such as laying fresh water-pipes . . . and that they were always

---

[5] Ecole des Hautes Etudes Commerciales.

[6] The table of references for the interviews is on p.60 ff.

having to appeal to a higher authority. The Ministers de Monzie and Loucheur intervened in support of Le Corbusier on repeated occasions. In fact, both here and in Marseille Le Corbusier received help from people in high places; this belies the impression given in his writings, where he claims to have encountered implacable opposition at all times.

At a local level, however, there really was opposition. According to Vrinat, every architect in Bordeaux was against the project:

> 'The architects of Bordeaux set up a general hue and cry;
> they criticized everything . . . As a result we found no
> purchasers for the houses. In 1930 I was engineer at the
> refinery, having replaced Frugès, who was suffering from
> a depression, and so I made the arrangements for the
> sale of the houses, in conjunction with Mme Frugès. The
> sale was eventually effected under the terms of the law
> enacted by Minister Loucheur . . . This law had the
> grave defect of not requiring the people [the future
> occupants] to make any financial contribution: all they
> had to do in order to benefit was fulfil the conditions
> laid down under the act. And so the families that went to
> live there were not very well off. They were the sort of
> people who simply never think of maintenance. For
> example, there is no sand on the terraces today, although
> it was provided when the houses were built, which also
> shows that the problems of waterproofing had been fully
> understood in the first instance . . .'

Doctor M., a municipal councillor during the construction period and shortly afterwards mayor of Pessac, was more or less representative of the opposition group:

> 'I had no confidence . . . it was strange, it broke with
> tradition . . . it was rumoured that these houses belonged
> to Abd-El-Krim . . . in their simplicity the people
> imagined that they were harems! . . . Public disaffection
> stemmed more from objections to the lack of amenities
> than from aesthetic disapproval . . . as far as the
> municipality was concerned, it always acted in a spirit of
> co-operation . . . true, I told Le Corbusier: "I prefer
> the Louvre" . . . but he was a fine type . . . a fine type! . . .
> we had our altercations but we always finished up by
> shaking hands . . .'

Despite this 'spirit of co-operation' the municipality virtually refused to allow water-pipes to be laid for several years. It was very difficult to find purchasers for the houses and by invoking the law passed by Minister Loucheur – which was specially modified to cover the Pessac project[7] the majority of the houses came to be occupied by people from a very low social stratum, many of whom subsequently often defaulted on their rent, despite the fact that this was extremely low. Meanwhile, the district degenerated more and more, due as much to the lack of upkeep as to social prejudice for, when they found themselves subjected to prejudice, the occupants developed little liking for maintenance.

As in Marseille, the *cité du fada*, so too in Pessac the external appearance of the houses prompted a number of pejorative sobriquets from the very outset – such as 'the Moroccan settlement' or 'the Sultan's district' – which will doubtless have played their part in turning the original occupants against their new homes:

> **F 3** — It was as if we had the plague: What! you live in the 'Moroccan district'! So I said to myself: Well now! what if I don't like it there? What am I going to do about it? . . . it was terrible! I felt as if I was being sent to prison . . .

Another sobriquet was prompted by Henry Frugès's interest in the sugar industry: 'Frugès's cubes of sugar'.

Since it drew on the international style, which was then in vogue and which Le Corbusier had helped to launch and propagate, the architecture of the Q.M.F. ran completely counter to the natural conservatism of the Bordeaux region, a fact which emerged quite clearly from local press comment at the time:

> 'In this region of Bordeaux, that is so rich in memories and *vieux crus*, it was a source of surprise and pleasure for us to see the dwelling of the future finally emerging from the earth . . .'

At the opening ceremony Minister de Monzie also stressed the natural conservatism of the region:

> 'It is a good and noble lesson that the Bordeaux region teaches us. One might perhaps have feared that it would not be overinclined to renew the great techniques

[7]This shows the importance attached to the experiment by the government.

of the past and so disrupt society, which is opposed to certain forms of boldness.'

This traditionalism was frequently evoked in the course of the interviews with the occupants and other local people.

> **M 3** — The people of Bordeaux are accustomed to 'lean-to' houses, they were thrown completely out of their stride.

This is perfectly true. In this region the people were, and still are, attached to a traditional and almost archetypal kind of dwelling: the *lean-to house*. We shall be considering the possible ramifications of this attachment on a later page. For the time being I merely wish to draw attention to a basic and curious phenomenon: if we compare the traditional lean-to house with the houses designed by Le Corbusier, we find that, although structurally completely different, they none the less resemble one another in one important respect, for they both lend themselves to conversion; and the conversion of the Pessac houses was, of course, the original motivating factor for our enquiry.

In lean-to houses conversion is a frequent, if not indeed, a regular feature. In fact, the appearance of this particular type of dwelling seems almost to be determined by this very process, whose unwritten laws appear to be well established, for it is invariably the back addition – in other words, the actual lean-to section of the structure – that gives these houses the asymmetrical roofs that are their most characteristic feature (see illustration 17). The internal features of the lean-to house are also determined by the back-addition: anyone in the Bordeaux region will tell you that a lean-to house is a single-storey dwelling set close to the road and consisting of a central corridor giving access to rooms on either side, the two inner rooms being dark in the majority of cases. Not that these dark rooms – which are typical of the internal layout of lean-to houses – were meant to be dark. What has happened is that the light provided by the original windows has been cut off by the incorporation of a back-addition. For since lean-to houses are mostly semidetached – and even when they are not the side elevations are usually windowless – the incorporation of a back-addition must necessarily deprive these inner rooms of their light.

But, quite apart from their undoubted flair for home conversions, the people of the Bordeaux region also reveal a marked propensity for filling the countryside with outbuildings, a practice which invariably arouses comment from those visiting the region for the first time. Consequently, the phenomenon of Pessac ought perhaps to be considered as symptomatic of a general tendency on the part of the local inhabitants to manage their household affairs in their own individual way. This observation strengthened me in my belief that the general implications of this tendency are of greater interest than the individual functional and other factors to which it is due.

The conclusions which I have drawn in respect of my method are set out in Chapter 4.

Finally, in order to round off this historical and geographical account of the project, I would like to draw attention to the original prospectus for the houses of the Q.M.F., which was issued with the express purpose of promoting sales and which has been reproduced as an appendix to this book. Apart from the information which it provides on the basic design of the houses, the tone of the prospectus is also extremely interesting.

By present-day standards the publicity for the Q.M.F. was totally misguided. Instead of reassuring prospective clients, it sowed doubts in their minds; and, although this was probably done deliberately in order to overcome apathy and force a response from the public, in the final analysis it merely served to underline the doubts entertained by the authors – Frugès and Le Corbusier – as to the commercial success of their project. In this it resembled the speech delivered by Frugès to the residents of the Q.M.F.

The first page of the prospectus is taken up by a photograph of one of the new houses with the following caption printed in bold type:

> **'the new look of this villa may
> perhaps raise doubts in your mind . . .'**

On the following page the caption continues in equally pessimistic terms:

> **'. . . as to its comfort and amenities
> you will ask yourselves whether
> traditional architecture does not
> offer you greater advantages than
> modern architecture.'**

In the course of this statement the doubt increases in intensity, the dubitative 'may perhaps' giving way to the affirmative 'you will ask yourselves'.

The authors also felt called upon to justify their decisions:

> 'The external appearance is not always pleasing at first
> sight; but experience has shown that the eye very soon
> grows accustomed to these *simple and pure forms* and,

before long, finds them more beautiful than the complicated and cumbersome forms found in sculptures and ornaments. For the past thirty years or so the objects of our day-to-day world have assumed extremely simple forms: clothes, tools and equipment, ships, motor-cars, etc. . . . and are not the simplest forms those with the most true flair, the most "class", the most bearing – in a word, the most beauty?
'And why should this not apply to our houses as well?
'All you have to do is ask the people who live in our villas how they feel about them and what it feels like to be living in them.'

'The Fascist state, which
will have to move quickly,
will choose a method
and institute a national
building policy.'
Le nouveau siècle
Article by Dr P. Winter

2
Contemporary press reaction

Most of the articles on the 'Quartiers Modernes Frugès' which appeared at the time were more or less stereotyped; they concentrated on the same motifs and revealed no real critical discernment. Whole passages in these articles appear to have been lifted straight from the writings of Le Corbusier. But are things any better today? Apparently not, for the motifs singled out by these earlier writers still seem to be very much in vogue . . . And we still find the same stereotyped approach.

(1) The housing crisis explained as a concatenation of circumstances.

'During the war all house-building projects were brought
to a halt whilst at the same time people's expectations
grew considerably under the impact of the stupendous
events which had thrown normal life into a turmoil
from 1914 to 1918.
'From 1918 onwards workmen, who would once have
been perfectly happy to find accommodation for
themselves and their – in some cases – large families
in a two-roomed flat, began to look forward to the day
when they would be able to order their lives more
agreeably in a small maisonette with 4 or 5 rooms.
Although perfectly natural, this desire was none the
less one of the salient features of social life in the
post-war period.' (*Petite Gironde*.)

(2) The need for serial production:

> 'The aim of modern building developments should be
> the provision of low rental accommodation. But, of
> course, low rental accommodation presupposes
> economic building methods: given the present cost of
> building materials, the idea of building an individual
> house or a group of houses treated as individual units
> on an economic basis is a delusion. Consequently, the
> time has come to consider the use of serial production
> methods in house building.' (*Petite Gironde*.)

(3) Attempts by industrialists to settle their labour problems.

> 'The only people to have used serial production
> methods on building sites are the industrialists, who
> were obliged to recruit personnel for their factories and
> discovered that, in order to attract the necessary
> labour force, they had to provide accommodation. But
> on numerous occasions the economy achieved by serial
> production resulted in poor living conditions and, in
> some cases, even impaired the structural stability of
> the houses.' (*Petite Gironde*.)

(4) The advantages accruing from the Pessac experiment: speed of work
and modern amenities.

> 'We encountered a completely novel aesthetic which
> seemed strange at first sight but to which our eyes soon
> grew accustomed.' (*Petite Gironde*.)

Here we find the arguments set out in the prospectus reproduced almost
verbatim. Incidentally, the local newspaper in Pessac itself – where
people were intimately concerned with the project – was more reserved
in its assessment of the aesthetic quality of the new houses:

> 'The highly unusual appearance [of these houses] –
> which from certain angles is reminiscent of the kind of
> houses built in our North African colonies – seems
> astonishing at first sight. But what does that matter,
> since modern amenities and perfect hygiene are the
> hallmarks of this new settlement. And if we have to
> make a choice, then dwellings built in this style – which
> admittedly is not calculated to inspire poetic dreams –

are preferable to the post-war 'slums' created in asymmetrical districts as a result of the growing practice of breaking up existing properties into smaller units.' (*La Tribune Pessacaise.*)

An allied theme, which was also frequently discussed, was that of the 'architectural laboratory'. This expression, which implies that the experiment is finished once the construction work has been completed, demonstrates the confusion between building and architecture that existed in the minds of contemporary critics.

It is hardly surprising, therefore, that architectural considerations as such should have been virtually non-existent in contemporary press reports. All we find is a long list of modern amenities: 'showerbath, washhouse, kitchen, wine and spirit storeroom, garden, terrace with flower beds, inner courtyard, poultry house, running water, electricity, central heating . . .' (*Mon Logis.*) Contemporary journalists also evinced a lively interest in the description of new building methods and concepts: serial production, tailorization, reinforced concrete, speed of work. But they seldom analysed the actual architecture; and on the rare occasions when such an analysis was provided, it was almost invariably a rehash of the arguments put forward by Le Corbusier in his own writings. An article under the significant title 'La machine à habiter', which appeared in a magazine called *Mon chez moi*, published by a managerial organization, is a case in point. In it the reviewer introduces highly condensed versions of passages from works by Le Corbusier, which eventually become so numerous that they virtually take over from the author, which is an interesting, if curious, method of procedure. The 'architectural laboratory' (the expression was coined by Frugès but was profitably incorporated into the publicity material for Le Corbusier's *Complete Works*), the 'machine to live in' (an expression, whose ambiguity will become apparent in the further course of this study) and all the other Corbusian clichés have provided the basis for innumerable articles of this kind. Where architectural matters are concerned, the general public shows a regrettable lack of discernment whilst the majority of journalists are no better. In this connexion it is worth noting that some forty years after the Pessac project an important French weekly that gave a detailed account of Le Corbusier's death, paying great attention to the melodramatic circumstances which surrounded it, was quite unable to provide an adequate review of his architectural œuvre, since no critical interpretation of his work had ever been published in the kind of language that would have been acceptable to its readers. This surely indicates that the general public still has but little rapport with architecture. As in the press reaction to the Pessac project, so too in this general review, we find what is virtually a transcription of different articles by Le Corbusier, which themselves were often repetitive. It would seem almost as if his ideas were so mystifying as to have completely suppressed any genuine spirit of enquiry on the part of popular writers.

But even in the specialist journals published at the time I was unable to discover a single critique or analysis of the architectural qualities of the Pessac project. Like many of the architectural reviews appearing today, they eschewed criticism in favour of factual presentation.

In this general dearth of original thought an article by Dr P. Winter, a member of the *Faisceau*, the Fascist group to which Le Corbusier is supposed to have belonged, stands out in sharp relief. Unlike the other writers of the times, he at least succeeded in illuminating one particular aspect of Le Corbusier's conception. His observations deserve to be quoted at length:

'Amongst the problems with which the Fascist state will have to deal as a matter of urgency, the problem of providing hygienic dwellings is one of the most important. We shall have to demolish all the slums in our towns. We shall have to rebuild, and our rebuilding programme will only be worth while if it is based on a detailed general plan evolved by people possessing a thorough knowledge of modern architectural methods. The *Faisceau* must take its stand here and now. The public bodies concerned with such matters must co-operate with one another in studying the various problems involved and must leave no avenue unexplored.

'The visit which we have made to the "Quartiers Frugès" in Pessac (near Bordeaux) has been highly instructive. In Pessac we have seen a new project, in which effective use was made of serial production methods in order to build low cost dwellings.

'M. Le Corbusier and M. Jeanneret, whose writings [see Le Corbusier, *Vers une architecture* (chez Crès)] are well known and whose strange pavilion dedicated to the *Esprit Nouveau* at the *Exposition des Arts Décoratifs* has aroused considerable comment, have been quite literally provided with an architectural laboratory at Pessac, thanks to the enthusiasm and initiative of M. Frugès. More than a hundred houses have already been built and the whole project is a great success. In this region of Bordeaux, that is so rich in memories and *vieux crus*, so traditionalist, it was for us a source of surprise and pleasure to see emerging from the earth the dwelling of the future, the kind of dwelling we had always wanted, the kind we had dreamt of but which we had thought was impossible at present . . . This project – take my word for it – was a fine stroke of audacity, and it was not achieved without great difficulty, without ambushes, because every innovator has to combat the prejudices not only of the small, but also of the great!

'M. Le Corbusier and M. Jeanneret have proved that their system is viable. The new "construction game" which they have evolved can be adapted equally well for town and country. We can already envisage new garden cities with their terraced villas and enormous skyscrapers, which will concentrate all industrial and working processes within a single, self-contained area far removed from the residential districts, which need a framework of vegetation, of peace and quiet, which need floriculture, playing fields near to hand and accessible at all times, in the open air, in front of the houses and on the roof gardens . . . Thanks to this new, simplified alphabet every individual will be able to build, according to his means, the house of his choice, from the most modest to the most grandiose. The system can be used to provide a well-designed farm for the educated countryman who has improved the yield of the land surrounding his dwelling . . .

'It can be used by the owner of a great estate or by an industrialist who wants to build a luxury villa for himself in some chosen setting. It can be used by everyone . . . both the smallest and the largest dwellings will be equipped with all the essential amenities and will provide the conditions necessary for maintaining health and promoting happiness and consequently for changing the life of the modern family in accordance with our precepts.

'The most remarkable aspect of this new system of building is perhaps the way in which the basic data were evaluated—in other words, its theoretical premise. Having developed the only really practical raw material for building purposes – reinforced concrete, which is cast by special methods and provides a rigid skeleton that is stronger than stone – man simply had to be creative. Armed with this new medium he had to

fashion a type of dwelling which would conform to his
ideal. He had to embark on a full-scale programme of
innovation, forgetting the ancient traditions, which
were imposed by the use of old materials, by old
prejudices and old ideas, and which have proved so
costly . . . He had to perform a veritable act of faith.
The choice of dimensions, the distribution of the rooms,
the exploitation of air and light were all dictated by
our needs, the needs of the twentieth-century family,
which must have well-lit rooms free from dark corners
and dust, rooms which provide the best possible basis
for physical well-being. Roof gardens with or without
canopies, houses above ground level with gardens
underneath . . . sun traps, running water, economical
central heating, showerbaths, WC's with septic tank
drainage, etc., etc. . . . The machine to live in is
complete. It can be extended at will to meet individual
needs, to meet the needs of the family which will live
in it . . . But, whatever the size, the component
elements are always the same . . . the organism with
all its elements, its cycle complete, useless remains are
disposed of, life leaves no trace, it does not hoard its
waste products, does not wallow in dirt and disease,
as is the case in the slums that we know only too well
. . . and that are inhabited by rich and poor alike.
'But, while serial production makes for low-cost
housing, it need not make for uniformity. With a
limited number of pawns a good chess player can
evolve endless permutations. And in Pessac, where
standard components were used throughout, no two
houses are alike. Each occupant will have the house of
his choice, built to suit his taste, his personality, his
feelings . . . The horrible rows of identical houses are
no longer necessary.
'The sense of unity created by the basic material and
the geometrical relationships established by the
component elements produce an extraordinary harmony
(and this is not purely fortuitous) – and the
architectural beauty of the structure emerges of its own
accord as the house takes shape. The layout of the
groups of houses, which takes due account of the
terrain and the massed vegetation, and the colour
schemes chosen for the outside walls ensure that the
complex harmonizes with the natural setting. There is

nothing offensive; these visionary but eminently habitable dwellings are taking their place in nature, without any sense of shock, without offending the eye, perfectly designed to fulfil their purposes . . . There was no need for complicated roofs, stylized timberwork, there are no gable ends, no turrets, no meaningless carvings, no blocks of hewn stone, no mosaic of brickwork . . . There is nothing but pure line; and that is a victory, a major rediscovery of simple designs and volumes.

'For many years now we have been living in a period of dead architecture, a period that has been dedicated to ugliness and waste because of the apparently invincible power of traditional values. Who amongst us is able to look at one of our modern monuments with its strange mixture of styles drawn from past eras without a feeling of revulsion? But we are all able to admire a beautiful motor-car, a steamship, a bridge, or a factory. In the same way, and with the same kind of emotion, we are able to admire the houses built by Le Corbusier and Jeanneret. The thing that strikes us most forcibly when we consider their project is that, above all, these two men are poets. Without grandiloquence, basing their work on simplified means and rigid principles (similar to the strict rules of prosody) and proceeding with painstaking economy they are contributing to the birth of a new aesthetic which reflects a spontaneous movement towards classical forms. They are inspired by a great feeling of hope and are entirely convinced of what they are doing. Today a man needs a good head for heights and a fair measure of cynicism if he is to succeed . . . if he is to build the Tower of Solness and make it stable, no matter how high it may be, without being overcome by vertigo and falling to an impotent death!

'But hasn't this all been done before?

'We know of other names, other projects . . . workers' settlements have been built before the one at Pessac . . . An architectural renaissance is underway, but of all the modern dwellings erected to date, none has been so well built or so well thought out, none has met the requirements of present-day living so fully, the essential requirements of health and hygiene . . . and none has been planned with such careful regard to cost effectiveness. Nobody has dared to use standardized components on such a scale.

'The Fascist state, which will have to move quickly, will choose a method and institute a national building policy. It should then be impossible for anyone to invoke the cause of liberty and democracy in order to erect slum dwellings, without effective sewage disposal, without modern amenities and without air or light, on individual building lots created by shameless speculators who parcel out good agricultural land for the sake of a quick profit and give a free rein to pasteboard follies which, in the final analysis, merely serve to augment our urban squalor.'

The general tone of this article and its underlying political ideas are so obvious that no comment is called for. As P. Francastel[1] has pointed out, 'Le Corbusier is a man of order. And for him order is to be found both in the inner logic of monumental systems and in social discipline.' But is there a definite rapport between these two types of order? Of course, Le Corbusier may have belonged to a Fascist group,[2] and he may have built the Central Soyuz in Moscow. But the fact that he has been accused of both Fascist and Bolshevist leanings would surely seem to indicate that one and the same building may be pressed into service as a standard bearer for different, even for diametrically opposed, ideas; and this would call into question the assumption that material and ideological orders are interrelated in the sense that they both belong to the one class.

Winter claims that 'more than a hundred houses have already been built and the whole project is a great success'. In fact, as we have already seen, the law passed by Minister Loucheur had to be specially amended in order to find occupants for the fifty-one houses at Pessac. But Winter's constant exaggeration is not the only point in his article that needs to be singled out. Certain expressions which he used also call for special consideration. For example, his statement that nobody *has dared to use standardized components on such a scale* and his reference to the *audacity* of the project should be considered in the light of the further statement that *he [Le Corbusier] placed his faith* in the concepts of organization, standardization and tailorization in which we also have *profound faith* (article in *Mon Logis*). Winter's observations would tend to bear out my own view of Le Corbusier's attitude to standardization.

[1] Pierre Francastel, *Art et Technique* (Paris, 1965).

[2] Francastel goes on to say: 'It should be pointed out that Le Corbusier showed immense dignity during the period when the partisans of a "new order" were occupying France . . . although he has been subjected to stringent criticism from certain quarters, this has left the loyalty and honour of the man unimpaired.'

Was it really the project that was standardized or was it the *modern family*, the 'twentieth-century family'? The use here of the generic singular form would certainly seem to imply a standardized family, whose living requirements were *so fully* understood: 'it [the system] . . . will provide the conditions necessary for maintaining health and promoting happiness and consequently for changing the life of the modern family *in accordance with our precepts*'. The only surprising thing here is that Winter does not speak of 'necessary and sufficient' conditions, which is what we might have expected. But Le Corbusier makes good the deficiency in his 'Conversations with Students of Architecture', where he speaks of forming 'the necessary and sufficient framework for a life that we are able to illumine . . .'

Finally, we must single out certain points in this article to which we shall be returning on a later page:

— the 'construction game', which will feature in the group discussion (where, however, it will be used in a modern context);

— the 'traditionalism' of the Bordeaux region, which is one of the principal factors in this enquiry;

— 'stability or strength' ('reinforced concrete, which . . . provides a rigid skeleton that is stronger than stone') ('pasteboard follies which, in the final analysis, merely serve to augment our urban squalor'), a factor which will be discussed in connexion with the interviews;

— the birth of a 'new aesthetic, which reflects a spontaneous movement towards classical forms', a paradoxical factor which is one of the characteristic features of the architecture of Le Corbusier, who was a traditionalist as well as a revolutionary.

'This is an example of
modern town planning, in
which historical mementoes
– such as the Swiss chalet
and the Alsatian "dovecote"
– have been left behind in
the museum of the past. A
mind stripped of Romantic
trammels tries to resolve a
problem that has been
precisely formulated . . .'
Le Corbusier

3
Le Corbusier's conception at Pessac

The architectural context

The period of modern architecture sometimes referred to as the 'heroic period' set in after the First World War. True, there were a number of early pioneers, such as Adolf Loos, who had given an impetus to the movement prior to 1920. But the really distinctive and decisive works of modern architecture were to emerge in the course of the 1920's and, more particularly, in the second half of that decade. The House of Rietveld in Utrecht dates from 1923, but Gropius's Bauhaus buildings and his project for a 'total theatre', Fuller's 'Dimaxion House', Alvar Aalto's library in Viipuri and his sanatorium in Paimio, and Mies van der Rohe's pavilion in Barcelona all saw the light of day towards the end of this period. The Pessac project was undertaken immediately prior to this last prolific phase.

Within Le Corbusier's own œuvre Pessac came just before the famous villa Savoye at Poissy and the villa de Garches (1927), the two really mature works which set the seal on the series of villas which he designed in the Paris region: villas in Vaucresson (1922), the villa of the painter Ozenfant in Paris (1922), maison La Roche-Jeanneret in Auteuil (1923), villa Meyer in Paris (1925) and maison Cook in Boulogne-sur-Seine (1926).

We see, therefore, that the Pessac project was conceived at a time when modern architecture had entered a particularly fruitful phase and when Le Corbusier himself had reached the peak of his first creative period. The ideas introduced by Le Corbusier in Pessac were not entirely his own. On the contrary, they were the product of an international movement. The merits of 'serial production' and 'standardization', for example, were being argued by other leading architects, including Gropius and Wachsmann. Such methods were also being advocated in France by architects such as André Lurçat.

Because of their technical and structural features the houses in Pessac are connected with what might be loosely called a 'Cubist aesthetic', which means of course that they were derived in the first instance from a comprehensive movement embracing all the arts. But, although Le Corbusier was pursuing a path of development that was not entirely individual, it is none the less profitable to compare his work with that produced by his contemporaries. The opportunity of doing so is furnished by the Weissenhof settlement built near Stuttgart in 1927 on the occasion of the *Werkbund* exhibition. There, within a single complex, we are able to study buildings designed by some of the greatest architects of the period, including Mies van der Rohe, Gropius, Scharoun, Oud, Behrens and Le Corbusier.

It is perhaps worth noting that Le Corbusier's work at Weissenhof was superior to that produced by the other members of this international group. However, I do not propose to discuss the relative merits of all the buildings designed for this project. I prefer instead to concentrate on the group of five terraced houses built by J. J. P. Oud, which lend themselves particularly well to a comparison with Le Corbusier's villas. Their dimensions (5 m × 10·50 m) are very close to those used at Pessac (5 m × 12·50 m), they have the same number of storeys and their general layout is essentially the same. Incidentally, a comparison was made at the time between Oud's Weissenhof houses and Le Corbusier's Pessac project in a German architectural journal (Wasmuth's *Monatsschriften für Baukunst*). It was not particularly favourable to Le Corbusier.

Although I do not wish to prejudge the issue, it seems to me that the essential difference between the two conceptions lies in the greater functionalism of Oud's design. In a monograph on Oud, Giulia Veronesi pointed out that in these houses he reached 'the peak of his "functionalist" development. Rigorously "rational", these interiors are amongst the purest of Oud's designs.'

This is perfectly true; every part of the available space was designed to function in a specific way and no part was required to perform more than one function. By comparison with this mechanistic arrangement, Le Corbusier's design appears far freer and far simpler: four squares, two measuring 5 m × 5 m and two 2·5 m × 2·5 m. If, for purposes of a more detailed comparison, we ink in on the two designs (on the opposite page) those areas destined specifically to serve as communication links, we find that the surface taken up in this way is far greater in Oud's design than in Le Corbusier's, where the upper landing on the staircase occupies only one square metre of space. Incidentally, in Oud's design the staircase is enclosed, which means that it fulfils a purely functional purpose, whereas in the Pessac design it is an open structure ascending from the living room, where it provides both a vantage point and a visual point of reference, thus contributing to the 'architectural promenade' so dear to Le Corbusier.

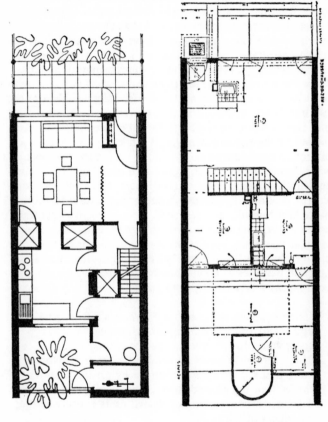

Oud's plan at Stuttgart   Le Corbusier's plan at Pessac

Functionalism

It is interesting to note that the theory of separate functions in urban development formulated by Le Corbusier is not reflected in his architecture, least of all in Pessac. His theoretical insistence on separate

31

spheres for 'living', 'working' and 'communications' had no tangible effect as far as the Q.M.F. were concerned. There we find virtually no corridors, no clear areas designed to serve exclusively as communications links. Oud's design, on the other hand, allowed for numerous elements of this kind, whose sole function was to enable the occupants to move from one part of the house to another and so gain access to the various rooms. (At this point the reader might perhaps think that I am confusing town-planning ideas with architectural ideas. However, we shall come to see that these two spheres are not as clearly delineated as is commonly supposed.) The conclusions I have drawn from the comparison of these two designs may appear subjective at first sight. In point of fact, however, my evaluation has a completely objective base, for it was evolved as a result of the interviews conducted in Pessac with the present occupants. And if we consider the architectural ideas in the light of these interviews we find that his current classification as a rationalist and functionalist architect is altogether too simplistic. One of the advantages of the enquiry was that it made it possible to assess the reality of architectural functionalism and to determine the *practical* implications for the occupants of a concept based on a theoretical classification. Significantly enough, some of those interviewed actually complained about the lack of rationalism, claiming that certain features of the houses were 'not logical', 'not rational', 'inconvenient', 'awkward' or 'impractical'. At first sight such criticism seems quite astonishing, considering that it was being applied to the man who had coined the expressions: 'a machine to live in' and 'a house-implement' . . . But if we examine certain passages in Le Corbusier's writings we find that his use of the word *machine* is decidedly ambiguous:

> 'The dictionary tells us that *machine* is a word of Latin and Greek origin meaning art or artifice: "a contrivance for producing specific effects" . . . which forms the necessary and sufficient framework for a life that we are able to illumine by raising it above the level of the ground through the medium of artistic designs, an undertaking dedicated in its entirety to the happiness of man . . .'

The ambiguity in this definition lies in the dual nature of the machine as a functional and a poetic object. On the one hand we have the technological and functional quality of what is 'necessary and sufficient' whilst on the other hand we have *effects*, *artifices* and *art*, all of which depend on the use of *designs* . . .

It would seem that, as far as the present occupants of Pessac are concerned, the artistic designs incorporated into the houses – and there were many of them – have lost any efficacy they may once have possessed: the transparent quality of the rows of terraces or of the 'arcades' at ground level really did constitute an 'effect' (see illustrations 22, 24, 26 which show the houses in their original condition), one that has now been completely destroyed as a result of the alterations. By the same token, the outside staircase leading from the first floor to the terrace (see illustrations 29–33), which was undoubtedly designed by Le Corbusier as a purely poetic element, is regarded by the occupants – and the passers-by – as an irrational and hopelessly impractical feature. None the less, Le Corbusier's poetic intention was clearly manifested in this instance. He himself wrote about this aspect of his work in a short article entitled 'A Small House', in which he commented on a villa that he had built during his Pessac period on the shores of Lake Geneva. His language is surprisingly simple: 'you go on to the roof, a pleasure that was enjoyed by certain civilizations in certain epochs'. In the same article we also find Le Corbusier's 'authentic facts of architecture': 'a plank serves as a bench, and behind, three horizontal gratings light the cellar. That can be enough to give pleasure (if you do not think so, move on!) . . .'

Serial production

The precise significance of 'functionalism' at Pessac was the first factor which called for elucidation within the general architectural context of the times.

But to my mind there was a second factor that was equally unclear: standardization. And here one is tempted to ask whether Le Corbusier was motivated by purely technical considerations or whether in fact he was not concerned also with ideological issues.

> 'By slow degrees the building sites will become industrialized,[1] and the incorporation of machines into the building industry will lead to the introduction of standard components; house designs will change, a new economy will be established; the standard components will ensure unity of detail and unity of detail is an indispensable condition of architectural beauty . . . Our towns will lose the look of chaos which disfigures them today. Order will reign and the network of new roads, which will be much wider and much more satisfactory from an architectural point of view, will provide us with splendid views. Thanks to the machine, thanks to

[1] *L'Almanach de l'Esprit Nouveau*, p.81.

standard components, thanks to selectivity, a new style will assert itself . . .'

The vision conjured up by Le Corbusier in this passage is not based on a lucid analysis of technical possibilities but on the same act of ethical and aesthetic faith which we have already encountered in a number of the press articles from which I have quoted. (Winter, for example, stated that 'nobody has *dared* to use standardized components on such a scale'.) Incidentally, it seems today, some forty years later, as if the industrialization of building 'by slow degrees' will not be possible. This is quite clear from the many setbacks that have been encountered. The fifty-one houses actually built at Pessac and even the 200 originally envisaged do not constitute a 'series' whilst the so-called 'series' of ten houses built at Lège was a complete misnomer. And when the short-comings of the system are hinted at in Le Corbusier's own writings, then it becomes quite apparent that standardization is being presented as an ideology and not as a technical innovation. (Strictly speaking, of course, twentieth-century standardization has not really been an innovation, for standard components have been used in building throughout the centuries. Bricks are a case in point.) The following passage, which first appeared in *L'Almanach de l'Esprit Nouveau* and in which Le Corbusier recorded a conversation that he had had with Frugès on the problem of standardization, throws considerable light on this matter:

'Standardization Cannot Resolve Architectural Problems.

Myself. — For every one of my houses and for every group of houses I have had to make detailed drawings on a scale of five centimetres to the metre. Extremely detailed and difficult, delicate. All the more detailed, delicate and difficult in that at Pessac we are working exclusively *with standard components:* the same windows everywhere, the same staircases everywhere, the same doors, the same heating, the same 5 m × 5 m or 2·50 m × 5 m concrete cells, the same kitchen and washroom equipment, the same dressing rooms.

M. H. Frugès. — But is that due to some shortcoming in the system of standardization, of serial production? It seems to me that, if everything has been standardized, then, provided the site foreman has been given precise instructions in the form of measurements or drawings, he should know where to site each house and where to place the windows.

Myself (and I have been struggling with such problems for the past year). — Yes, it is a shortcoming in the system of standardization! Although it may also be its salvation! A work [of architecture] cannot express emotion or touch our inner sensitivity unless its form has been dictated by a genuine intention. And Mr X (whom neither of us knows but who will one day become the owner of one of these houses) will only respond to that intention if we have invested it in the building. This intention is the care that we will have taken to entice him on to this little plot of ground by giving him all the good light that he needs, by excluding harmful draughts from his house, by planting his flowers and his fruit trees in the sun, siting his kitchen with expertise, fitting his front door in plumb and facing the garden path, placing his windows to provide a good view, his bedroom where he will not be overlooked by the neighbours, etc., etc. . . . If we did not spend such loving care on each house, we would be turning out miners' cottages, in which case our system of serial production and standardization would have failed because the dwellings would not be good to live in. Standard components are letters; with those letters, and in a particular way, you have to spell out the names of your future house owners.'

This last sentence contains the whole kernel of Le Corbusier's architectural conception for Pessac. One might, of course, be justified in thinking that the future occupants had also subsequently taken the trouble to write their own names *in their own way* . . .

But what is quite clear from this passage is that, as far as Le Corbusier was concerned, standardization was meant to apply to the structural components and not to the actual house. However, when we move into the sphere of town planning (and Pessac is an example of modern town planning) the situation becomes more complex, for in this sphere houses are themselves components. By varying the relative positions of his standard components (see illustration overleaf) Le Corbusier claimed that he was able to achieve, not only variety, but also individuality:

'Rational construction based on the use of component blocks does not destroy individual initiative.'

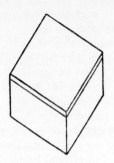 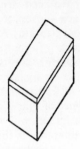 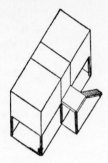

1 cell ½ cell 2 cells

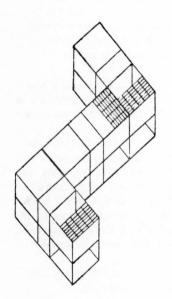 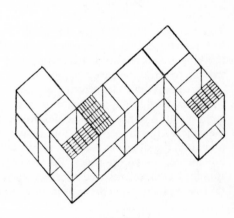

Principle of standardization
(see illustrations 26 and 27)

36

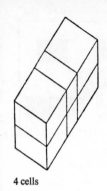

4 cells

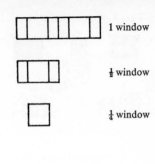

1 window

½ window

¼ window

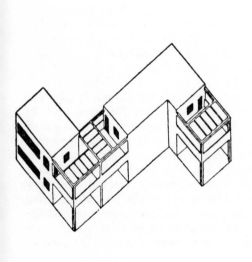

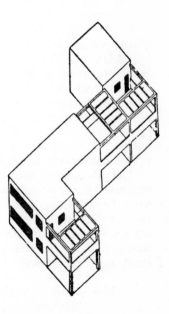

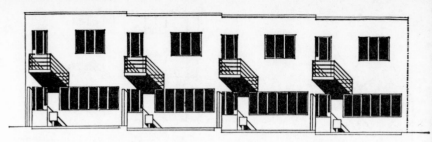

Terraced houses built by J. J. P. Oud in the Weissenhof
settlement near Stuttgart. 1927. Compare this façade with
Le Corbusier's (illustration 18)

From architectural layout to urban composition

We must now consider the layout and the individuality of Le Corbusier's houses.

Here again it is interesting to compare Le Corbusier's ideas with those developed by J. J. P. Oud. At Stuttgart, Oud placed identical houses in juxtaposition so that the only way of distinguishing between them was by the slightly irregular alignment of the façades. In another project – the 'Kiefhoek' district in Rotterdam – he went so far as to design completely undifferentiated façades, many of which extend for as much as 100 metres, with the result that there is no possible way of telling which section of the façade corresponds to which house. The originality of Le Corbusier's Pessac project lies in the use of what might best be described as an alternating façade, in which every other house is turned back to front and which ensures that each individual house is readily distinguishable from its neighbours. Thus, differentiation is achieved by effecting 'positional' variations of absolutely identical components. But this variation is not restricted to the façades, i.e. to the exterior of the houses, for Le Corbusier also isolated each pair of houses in functional terms. And so, as a result of this alternating system, we find, for example, that a bedroom in one house is juxtaposed to the terraces in the two neighbouring houses. This means that it is isolated from the neighbours' bedrooms which, since they fulfil the same function, would presumably be used at the same time. By juxtaposing living areas which served different purposes – bedroom/terrace or dining-room/patio – Le Corbusier achieved a high degree of isolation, both physically and psychologically, to which the occupants did not fail to respond.

> **M 3** — You see, it's intimate! . . . You don't hear the tenant next door and he doesn't hear you, because it's all vice versa . . .

> **F 10** — It's good because you never hear anything: if I have

38

guests, the sound of our voices will carry towards the garden, if the lady next door has guests, their voices will carry towards the road . . .

F 3 — This system of having one house facing the front and the other facing the back, I find that very good because you never have trouble with your neighbours; when I'm in my kitchen at the back, my neighbour is in her kitchen at the front . . . I go out at the back to my dustbins and so on, and she – she goes out the front . . . you know, we often spend a whole day at home without seeing one another . . . Although we're all packed together like this, you still have the feeling that you're on your own . . .

Clearly, Le Corbusier's attempt to achieve isolation was highly successful at a psychological level. If an occupant 'has the feeling' that she is on her own, that is all that is needed, since for all practical purposes the feeling of isolation is the same as actually being isolated. In a limited survey which we carried out in a town composed of traditional terraced houses we discovered that although the houses were undoubtedly isolated from one another in the physical sense, the householders did not feel themselves to be isolated. This is the only rational explanation for the different and often contradictory answers they gave when asked whether living in a terraced house posed any noise problems: some said they could not hear their neighbours at all and were not disturbed in any way, others said they could hear everything: showerbath, television, even arguments.

Terraced houses with party walls have considerable advantages – they save space, keep down building costs and are easily heated. But they pose one major problem: acoustics. And by the simple expedient of reversing every other house Le Corbusier provided a remarkable solution to this problem.

Ordinarily, the problem of isolation, which is essentially of a technical order, would have been dealt with by the application of soundproof materials. In Pessac, however, it was effectively resolved by the introduction of a new type of architectural layout. Of course, this architectural design also resulted in a new form of urban composition. Thus, what at first sight had appeared to be a purely technical problem prompted a solution involving the relationship between the individual and the collective; this lies at the heart of our enquiry.

Le Corbusier's solution to the problem of isolation can be taken at three different levels: as a technical device, as an architectural feature and, at the highest level, as an example of urban composition. In this particular instance architecture and town planning go hand in hand.

We must now consider the *kind* of town planning advocated by Le Corbusier.

Since they were conceived as self-contained units the *unités d'habitation* can scarcely be regarded as urban clusters. (The fact that Le Corbusier himself always regretted not having been able to build groups of *unités* would suggest that he too would have subscribed to this assessment.) Consequently, the only town-planning projects that Le Corbusier completed were those at Pessac and Chandigarh. True, anyone who takes this view has to accept that fifty-one houses (out of a projected 200) constitute an urban cluster whilst 320 flats do not . . . The distinction is paradoxical but, for this very reason, perfectly reflects Le Corbusier's attitude towards town planning, for from the very beginning of his career he vacillated between two completely opposite conceptions. The first of these, derived from the horizontal structures of the garden city, found expression in his designs for the 'Maisons Monol', whilst the second, which depended on high density vertical structures, formed the basis for his plan for Paris of 1925. Here we find the classical antithesis between collectivism and individualism which, in the final analysis, determines all town-planning problems, no matter what they are concerned with: fittings, property, aesthetics, legislation, etc. . . . And it was precisely this antithesis that Le Corbusier tried to resolve by combining extreme isolation with extreme communality in his *unités d'habitation*.

Although it was derived from the opposite conception, namely the *garden city*, the Pessac project marked the first fruits of the high density solution achieved in the *unités d'habitation*. And if the sponsor of the Pessac development, M. Frugès, a man with a forceful personality, had not disagreed with Le Corbusier in this respect because, as he himself explained, he wanted to 'offer the workers houses that were fully detached', then we would undoubtedly have seen at Pessac examples of the *immeubles-villas* which Le Corbusier had first conceived in 1922. Both architecturally and linguistically these *immeubles-villas* were the perfect expression of the antithesis between the individual and the collective and for this reason they continued to engage Le Corbusier's attention until he eventually found a solution to this problem with his *unités d'habitation*.

In the end Frugès and Le Corbusier agreed on a combination of semi-detached houses arranged in different groupings of twos and threes, some small terraces of five or six houses each and a few detached houses. And here again we come up against the problem of standardization. It could of course be argued that this problem is simply an alternative form of the antithesis between the individual and the collective: although a collective system has to be adopted – for both economic and structural reasons – it need not prevent the architect from achieving

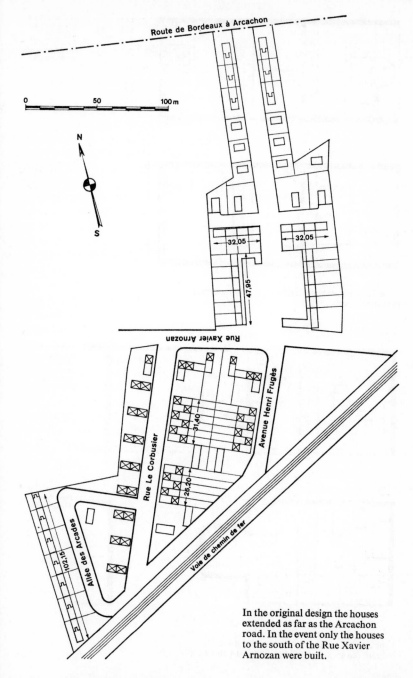

In the original design the houses
extended as far as the Arcachon
road. In the event only the houses
to the south of the Rue Xavier
Arnozan were built.

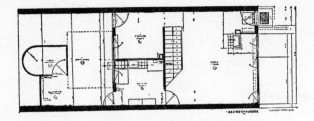

Ground floor:
living room,
kitchen,
room,
washhouse and
wine cellars

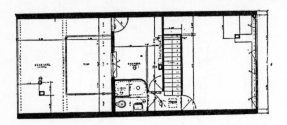

First floor:
large bedroom,
small bedroom,
dressing room
and terrace

Type 1: two-storeyed, terraced house with terrace
(see illustrations 18–27)

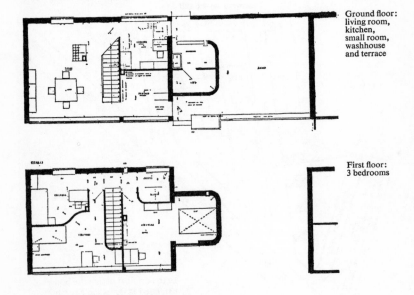

Ground floor:
living room,
kitchen,
small room,
washhouse
and terrace

First floor:
3 bedrooms

Type 2: with arcades and terraces at ground level
beneath the arcades (see illustrations 14 and 44–47)

42

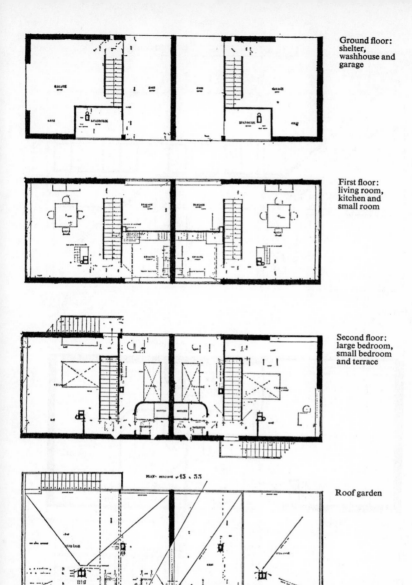

Ground floor:
shelter,
washhouse and
garage

First floor:
living room,
kitchen and
small room

Second floor:
large bedroom,
small bedroom
and terrace

Roof garden

Type 3: semidetached at ground-, first- and
second-floor levels with access to third-floor
roof garden via outside staircase
(see illustrations 12 and 28–41)

43

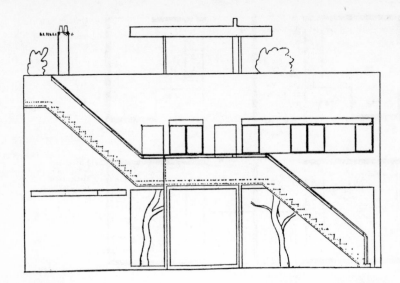

Elevation

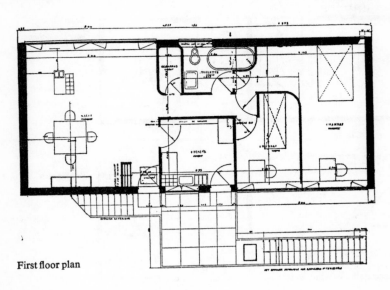

First floor plan

Type 4: two-storeyed, detached with access to
second-floor terrace via an outside staircase
(see illustrations 48–54)

44

individuality. On the contrary, it may well help him to do so. Moreover – as we have already seen – standardization in Pessac was not motivated by technical considerations alone; it also served to justify an ideology which appears to have been based on town-planning conceptions.

Architecture and dwellings

But an even more fundamental facet of Le Corbusier's conception than any of the factors we have discussed so far was the fact that he wanted to 'produce architecture' by building houses. Although we will be dealing with the more detailed ramifications of this notion in a later chapter it is perhaps worth mentioning that, at that time, very few people thought of dwelling houses as proper subjects for architecture.

> 'You know, at the Ecole des Beaux-Arts in Paris,[2] which is one of our biggest architectural institutes, dwellings have never formed part of the curriculum. No attention has been paid to the things that make up the lives of all human beings: everyday things, the moments and the hours passed day in and day out, from childhood till death, in rooms, square, simple places, which can be moving, constituting as they do our primordial theatre, where we act out our feelings from the moment we open our eyes on the world. In 1920, when we created *L'Esprit Nouveau*, I established the fundamental significance of dwelling houses by describing them as "machines to live in" ... An exclusively human programme, placing man once again in the centre of architectural creation ... dwelling– town-planning, a twin concept that is quite indispensable ... when it is devoted to dwellings, architecture is an act of love, not a *mise en scène* ...'

It seems that Le Corbusier's insistence on introducing architectural qualities into his houses was the chief reason for the astonishment evinced by the occupants when first confronted with his work:[3]

> **M 8** — That chimney ... it is both well sited and badly sited ... a chimney in the middle of a room, I find that disturbing ... and yet it is well sited because ... because it not only provides a chimney, it also provides a corridor ... and, you know, you get used to it ... and when you're used

---

[2] 'Conversation with Students from the Schools of Architecture', 1943.
[3] See Chapter 5: Group Discussion.

to it, you don't look at it in the same way . . . at first it was rather disturbing: I mean, a staircase in the middle of a room, it's odd . . . and the kitchen is also badly sited because it's opposite a hall so you can't see anything . . . it's good and bad, it's disturbing . . . *there are some things which don't seem to be in the right place . . . and yet they . . . they are there. That's what's . . . that's what's good, precisely that!* . . . but the staircase, now I find that is in the right place, because like that, flanking the dining-room, it has the effect of separating the two rooms without having a wall, *it's good . . . and it's not good at one and the same time . . . and that's what's good about it.*

PART TWO

'When considering propositions based on probability we usually find that any one proposition is opposed by another which appears equally plausible. From a scientific point of view, therefore, it would be just as profitable to take two such plausible opinions and try to determine which of the two actually does conform to reality as to advance an entirely new conception of reality. This is the precise difference between scientific knowledge and popular knowledge . . .' Halbwachs

4
Method

Although I have occasionally found it necessary to exceed the spatial and temporal limits of the Pessac project, this project was sufficiently restricted in itself – both geographically (size of the site) and numerically (number of houses on the site) – to make this an essentially limited study. Nonetheless, although the study itself is limited, the questions which it raises are extremely far-reaching.

In so far as it was a *garden city* Pessac might well have inspired a study based on the antithesis between town and country, a theme that was frequently broached by the occupants during the interviews. It could also have been investigated in terms of the antithesis between the individual and the collective, an approach that would have been facilitated by the separation of the dwellings into semidetached and terraced houses on the one hand and detached houses on the other. Another possibility would have been to consider Pessac in the light of its importance as part of Le Corbusier's architectural œuvre or even in terms of the standardization and industrialization of building techniques which, in view of the housing crisis of modern times, constitute one of the key aspects of twentieth-century architecture.

However, there are numerous questions of a more detailed nature which would arise no matter which approach was adopted:

Are the people of Pessac capable of responding to standardization and do they regard it as a personalizing factor? Is there a latent need in man to alter his home? Do the occupants respond to the poetic aspect of architecture when this is manifested in their homes? Do different social classes have different attitudes to architecture? When they made

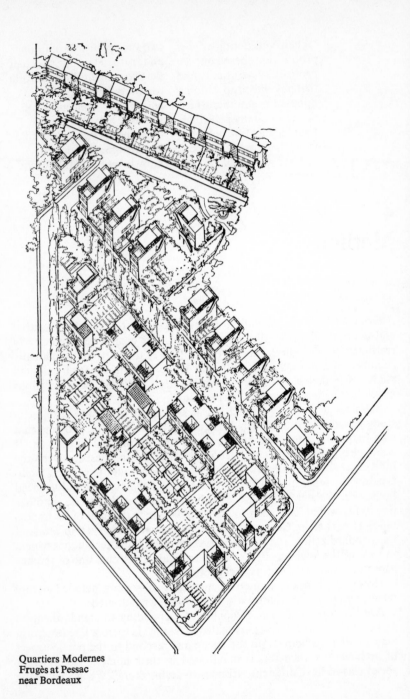

Quartiers Modernes
Frugès at Pessac
near Bordeaux

50

Pessac 1925. M. Frugès said to us: 'I authorize you to put your theories into practice and to carry them to their most extreme conclusions; I wish to achieve really conclusive results in the field of low-cost housing: Pessac must be regarded as a laboratory. I authorize you to break with all conventions and abandon traditional methods. In a word: I am asking you to tackle the problem of designing a house, to establish suitable forms of standardization, to build walls, floors and roofs to high standards of strength and durability and to introduce a full system of tailorization by the use of machines, which I authorize you to purchase. You will equip and design the interiors of these houses so as to make them easy and pleasant to live in. As for any aesthetic quality that may result from your innovations, this should have nothing in common with the aesthetic quality of traditional houses—which are costly to build and costly to maintain—but should reflect the contemporary epoch. The purity of the proportions will provide you with your most eloquent testimony.'

[The story of] Pessac is rather like a Balzac novel. A generous man wants to show his country that it is possible to solve the housing problem. Public opinion is disturbed; jealousies are roused; the building firms, from the smallest local contractor to the architects, are worried about the new methods, which could destroy the positions they have acquired. And so, little by little, an atmosphere of hostility is created. The village of Pessac was built in less than a year by a Paris firm, which took over from various groups of local workers who had proved inadequate to the task. However, once the structural work had been completed—in 1926 —we encountered considerable opposition from the local administrative departments, which were supposed to expedite our application for connection to the main sewer and, subsequently, for the laying of water-pipes in the village. But, although we were granted permission to sell or rent the houses, we received no other authorizations. *Three years later*, in the spring of 1929, *the papers had still not been signed and the village was still unoccupied.* And this despite the fact that two government ministers took a personal interest in the project and both paid official visits to Pessac. M. de Monzie, the Minister of Public Works, came in 1926; M. Loucheur, the Minister of Labour, came in 1929. But the enthusiasm which had set in following the ministerial visit of 1926 gradually gave way to anxiety and, three years later, the press in various countries was reporting that *nobody could live in Pessac because it had been built on faulty principles.* In the end, thanks to the energetic intervention of M. Loucheur, an enquiry was instigated, which got to the bottom of this disturbing affair and discovered the reasons for the lack of water. This is a sad and bitter lesson, one which deserves to be recorded in the annals of the 'Idea' and which shows that new initiatives are an affront to public opinion and that public opinion makes war on ideas.

Document reproduced from 'Le Corbusier et Jeanneret deux confrères 1910–1929' (Zurich).

their modifications did the occupants actually produce architecture? – etc., etc.

Instead of restricting this study to the analysis of one particular aspect of the Pessac experiment I have kept it as wide as possible so as not to have to sacrifice the universal quality of 'living' as revealed by the day to day activities of the occupants; and I have tried to compare 'living', conceived in these terms, with architecture which, as an essentially synthetic discipline, is required to integrate the various technical, aesthetic and human factors involved in the building of houses.

I decided that the best way to proceed with the enquiry was to carry out a series of non-directive interviews. However, of the 174 people living in the district we were able to interview only a certain proportion, for a variety of reasons. Some simply were not at home when we called whilst others refused point blank to co-operate with us; this – as we shall see – was not without its significance. Moreover, we discovered that our frequent appearances in the district, which had aroused the curiosity of the householders at first and so had helped us in our enquiries, eventually became a tedious routine for a certain group of residents, who spent a large part of their day looking out of the window. Others were told by their neighbours about our project and by the time we came to speak to them were no longer very interested in giving us their impressions. All in all, we interviewed some forty persons. Our selection was determined by various factors, such as the type of house, the existence or absence of modifications, the status (tenant or owner) of the householders and their length of residence in the district, the age of the occupants and the size of the families in different houses. The data contained in the census of 1962, which was carried out by the I.N.S.E.E., (Institut National de Statistiques et d'Etudes Economiques) enabled us to form a general idea of the social and professional classes represented in the Q.M.F.

There were certain questions which seemed to us to arise quite spontaneously, and it was virtually impossible not to form preconceptions about the developments which had taken place in Pessac or to formulate theories to account for the changes to which the district had been subjected. But this made it all the more important not to hint at such theories in the interviews, for we had to create a framework – without bringing any influence to bear – that would enable the occupants to think about their houses and recall their experiences. By doing this we would also be lending greater significance to the presence or absence in the interviews of any set questions and to the way in which these were formulated. Moreover, in so far as such questions were capable of elucidating the kind of approach adopted by the architect to the problems of architecture and living, I thought it might be interesting to draw up a list so that they could then be debated. This was done in the group discussion, for which we were joined by five architects with different basic outlooks. A further object of the group discussion was to consider the Pessac project in the light of Le Corbusier's personality.

We also conducted a historical enquiry in the Bordeaux region and were able to interview some of the people serving on the town council during the construction period. (This enquiry was reinforced by a careful study of articles which had appeared at the time both in the local press and in specialist journals on the problems of architecture and living.)

I received more detailed information on the development of the project from M. Vrinat, who had been in charge of the construction work, and M. Frugès. As a result of my contacts with the latter I came to appreciate the strength of his personality and to realize the importance of the contribution he had made by enabling Le Corbusier to test his ideas, which had, of course, met with his enthusiastic approval. An industrialist by profession – but not by inclination – Frugès took a keen interest in the arts. But for this fortuitous combination of talents, which made him an ideal patron, Pessac could scarcely have been built.

In the course of the historical enquiry I discovered that the French television service had visited Pessac at the time of Le Corbusier's death and had returned there in February 1967, when the mayor had applied for the district to be classified as a historical monument. This was an important factor, which had to be taken into consideration in assessing the observations recorded during the interviews, which must have been influenced to some extent by these events.

Moreover, on 19 June 1966 a special ceremony was held to commemorate the fortieth anniversary of the 'Quartiers Modernes Frugès', at which both M. Frugès, who was guest of honour, and M. Vrinat spoke about the development of the project to an audience which included the present-day residents of the Q.M.F. These residents will doubtless also have read the press reports of Le Corbusier's death, which received nationwide coverage. It is possible, therefore, that the attitudes they expressed may have been rather different than they would have been had the interviews taken place prior to these events. Once they realized that Le Corbusier was a well-known and respected figure, some of the occupants were obviously inclined to modify their opinions; they hesitated to think their true thoughts or to say what they really wanted to say:

> M 7 — Now that he's dead, people recognize his qualities . . .
> you have to realize that his ideas are now being applied
> everywhere: low ceilings, terraces, small kitchens, huh . . .

In France a man has to wait till he's dead to receive recognition! . . . I see that some new blocks have just been built over there on the Arcachon road, and they're in the same style. The UNESCO building . . . I believe he built it . . . drew up the plans and everything, didn't he! . . . and when they had the earthquake in Agadir, he wanted to rebuild Agadir . . . *in his own style, of course . . . a little personal perhaps for those times, but now I see that it's being taken up again* . . . the terraces, I see they're being built everywhere now . . .

F 15 — Well I don't know . . . this settlement was built at the request of M. Henry Frugès, but I don't know if all of Le Corbusier's settlements have been built in that style . . . this was done at the request of a person who expressed certain wishes, who said: 'I want something in this particular style' or 'Submit designs for my staff, I will study them' . . . I've heard all the people on the radio and television singing Le Corbusier's praises, apparently he has done absolutely marvellous things in other countries . . . and in France there's nothing . . . with the possible exception of Marseille . . . although it seems there are pros and cons about that too; because I've heard people who've come here from Marseille and who say it's . . . outstanding . . . and others who say: 'It's absolutely atrocious and even modern buildings would be preferable', although when it comes to that, Marseille is modernistic too . . . So, opinions differ . . . In India, on the other hand, it seems that . . . of course, the people there don't live the way we do, the people in India and Brazil . . . I don't know . . . you see, I don't know what the men who designed these houses thought it would be like to live in them . . . and then, you'd want to know what the houses were like when they were handed over to the workers who first lived in them; and I'm not so sure about that because . . . I've been told . . . they didn't always follow the architect's plans although, to be honest, I don't know whether that's true or not . . .

M 9 — He did that . . . it was . . . his own conception, hm . . . I don't know whether Le Corbusier . . . hm . . . always designed things like that . . . perhaps it was the building contractor who took it upon himself . . .

If they did not like it, then the fault could not possibly lie with Le Corbusier: after numerous detours they finally got round to saying that 'there are certain things which – in my opinion – are not good', and for this they blamed 'the men who designed these houses' but never 'Monsieur Le Corbusier'.

In this initial series of non-directive interviews, which constituted the first stage of our enquiry, we spoke to forty individuals or small groups for about one and a half hours each, recording our conversations on tape. All of these interviews were held in Pessac, although one of them was with a group of people who lived about 5 kilometres from the Q.M.F. They had heard a lot of local comment about the district during the construction period, had seen it on various occasions whilst on bicycle rides but had not been near it for the past five years. This particular interview was concerned primarily with the 'architect'.

The results of our initial enquiry proved so interesting that I decided to conduct the rest of the study along similar lines, using non-directive interviews and dispensing with questionnaires. It would, after all, have been a pity to have thrown away the considerable advantages offered by the non-directive method in order to obtain precise answers on isolated points which were, as it happens, more isolated than interesting. Moreover, any answers given to specific questions of this kind would almost inevitably have been subject to a certain reserve, especially those to questions involving the personality of Le Corbusier or the suggested classification of the villas as historic monuments (a suggestion which the occupants found quite astounding). Even when we asked quite simple questions on specific points – for example, whether the occupants made use of their terraces – we received evasive replies, a tendency which would have been far more pronounced had we employed a set questionnaire, however loosely framed. The following excerpt from one of the interviews illustrates this point:

    a — Do you use your terrace from time to time?

    F 6 — Huh!... well yes, we go up there ... it's very pleasant... you get a good view from up there ...

    a — You set out chairs for yourselves?

    — Well, you know ... we don't go up there much ... we do go ... of course. But ...

    a — But you're glad you've got it?

> — That's it! . . . we're glad we've got it, besides we can always slip out up there; if we're upstairs and don't want to come down, we can get a breath of air on the terrace . . .

If we had used standard questionnaires in the interviews we would have lost a great deal. Statements like these, for example:

> **F 10** — *Apart from that* these houses are all right . . .
> or
> — *None the less* there is a living room in these houses . . .
> — there is *none the less* a . . . there is *none the less* . . .

During this second phase of the enquiry the interviews were appreciably shorter, for there was no need to dwell at length on the issues already covered in the earlier interviews. They were also more numerous and dealt more fully with the external appearance of the new district. During this phase we were able to make a number of useful comparisons for we interviewed the people living in some of the more traditional houses overlooking the Q.M.F and also spoke to the residents of a new settlement built in 1960 not far from Pessac, which consisted of terraced and semi-detached houses that had more than one point in common with Le Corbusier's villas. There was one particularly interesting interview with a lady who had previously lived in her own house in the Q.M.F.; she still owned this house and was seriously considering whether to move back into it.

It goes without saying that the people we interviewed belonged to various age groups and – within the general limits imposed by the social status of the community – various professional categories. They had also lived in the district for varying lengths of time.

Because of the significance attached to the traditional character of the Bordeaux region by the press we decided that we would try to draw out a number of the people we spoke to on the subject of the 'lean-to' house, a type of dwelling which, as we have seen, is very common in that part of France.

Whilst conducting the interviews we also made a close scrutiny of the condition of the various houses to which we gained access. The points that interested us here were: the layout of the interior, the alterations (or lack of alterations), the furnishings and the cultivation of the gardens. In certain circumstances the lack of alterations could be just as significant as the alterations themselves. The redeployment – without structural alterations – of the interiors and even the names given to certain living areas were also revealing.

Most of the conclusions that I drew were based on the results of the interviews combined with our own observations.

Finally, we paid particular attention both to the actual sites and to the position of the houses on the sites, which I have subsumed under the generic term 'situation'. In view of the fact that standardization had been employed, it was of course eminently practical, 'all other things being equal', to study the siting of the houses. But it was not only practical, it was also extremely interesting, for by their very nature standard components tend to make for uniformity and so force the architect to seek new ways of introducing variety. (In this connexion it is worth recalling Le Corbusier's definition of such components as letters with which 'you have to spell out the names of your future house owners'.) I had always assumed that there might conceivably be a connexion between the siting of particular houses on the one hand and the personalities and style of living (including any penchant for alterations) of their occupants on the other. This assumption was borne out by the first series of interviews.

Both in our analysis of the non-directive interviews and in the directions we gave to certain controlled interviews, three factors were studied in great detail:

(1) The *alterations* or, to be more precise, the particular type of interior arrangement adopted by the occupants.

(2) The *composition* of the various types of houses as conceived by Le Corbusier on the basis of standard components.

(3) The relative *positions* and the sites of the houses in the district.

In assessing the implications of these three factors I was helped to a considerable extent by the fact that they constituted three variables which could be related to the constant factor of standardization. The different types of houses designed by Le Corbusier were, of course, all based on this constant, as were the alterations effected by the householders. Moreover, it was by playing about with his 'standard cells', his 'standard dominoes', that Le Corbusier created the urban composition of the whole district. In all three cases the standard components represented a system of reference and provided the fixed co-ordinates on which the variations were based.

Approaching the occupants

In order to ensure that the interviews would be as non-directive as possible we told the occupants in nearly all cases that we were carrying out a general architectural study, of which Le Corbusier's project constituted just one aspect. This approach achieved its object, as is evident from the following excerpt from one of the interviews:

M 19 — It would be interesting to know precisely what he [Le
Corbusier] had in mind . . . you know . . . at the outset,
and to see the way in which the people . . . incidentally, it
would make a good subject for an enquiry . . . a system-
atic study . . . of the way in which a house is transformed
by its occupants, I think it would be very interesting to
see what they've done, why they've done it, and so on . . .

This interviewee, who was well versed in sociology, was advising us to
do the very thing we were in fact doing . . .

Note on the presentation of the interviews

It goes without saying that, in general, the most profitable way of analysing an interview is by comparing passages with other passages in that interview or with passages from other interviews.

This method of procedure, which is especially advantageous in that it also affords the reader ample opportunity to make his own comparisons, makes for continuous reproduction. By and large the exposition in this study is continuous. Consequently, it stresses the guideline (in other words, the author's interpretation), which is occasionally non-linear and dichotomous, and so inevitably involves a certain amount of repetition. In particular cases, however, we have opted for continuous reproduction rather than continuous exposition. This dual approach naturally raised certain problems of presentation, which we have solved in the following way:

- — The extracts from the interviews have been set in from the margin of the text and are, therefore, clearly discernible;
- — The interviews have been numbered according to the code set out in the reference table at the end of this chapter, which also gives the approximate age of the interviewees and lists the pages on which extracts from their interviews appear;
- —**O** before a numeral means that the interviewee lives outside the Q.M.F.;
- —**N** before a numeral means that the interviewee lives outside the Q.M.F. but in a neighbouring street;
- **F** indicates that the interviewee is female;
- **M** indicates that the interviewee is male;
- **C** indicates that the interviewee is a child (under 15 years of age);
- **s** — indicates that the interview was conducted by the sociologist;
- **a** — indicates that the interview was conducted by the architect (author);
- **s** — . . . and **a** — . . . indicate an intentional silence on the part of the interviewer;
- — Words or phrases emphasized by the interviewees have been reproduced in **bold** print;
- — Words or phrases which the author wishes to emphasize have been printed *in italics*;
- — Explanatory remarks by the author have been printed in [square brackets].

Reference table for the interviews

No	Age (approx.)	Remarks	Pages on which extracts from the interviews appear
F 1	40		82
M 1	40		13, 105, 116, 122, 123, 138
M 2	55		74, 94, 105, 137, 140
M 3	65	Original occupant	16, 38, 84, 87, 88, 89, 92, 94, 105, 117, 138
F 3	65	Original occupant	15, 39, 81, 88, 94, 109, 140
OM 4	65	Original occupant now living elsewhere but thinking of returning	
M 5	45		
F 6	65	Original occupant	55, 81, 87, 88, 89, 94, 120, 126, 129, 138, 158
M 7	40		53, 85, 99, 100, 145, 146
M 8	18	Has always lived in Pessac	45, 98, 101, 108, 126, 156
F 9	65		
M 9	65	Original occupant who knew Le Corbusier	54, 82
F 10	30	Housewife with one child. Now living in her second house in the district	38, 56, 110, 114, 122, 158
F 11	40		
F 12	35		
F 13	60		80, 82
M 13	20		82, 120
M 14	65		77, 90
M 15	30		85, 158
F 15	30		54, 83, 95, 100, 104, 105, 118, 134
F 16	70	Original occupant	
M 17	40		
M 18	40		95
M 19	35	Junior lecturer at the University	57, 74, 96, 103, 111, 112, 116, 126, 136, 147
M 20	40	Works at home	96, 114, 148, 149, 150, 151
F 20	40		96, 97
M 21	40	Serving with the forces	145
M 22	35	Librarian	73, 112, 116
M 23	70	Original occupant	
F 24	70		
M 25	70	Original occupant	
F 25	70	Original occupant	
OM 26	40	Parisian, staying with a local family	159
NF 27	65		138
NM 28	70		
OF 29	45		119
OM 30	40		119, 154, 155
OM 31	40		
OF 32	40		91, 154, 155
OF 33	40		91, 98, 135
OC 34	15		119
OF 35	60	Had heard about the district	81, 84, 85, 90, 95, 97, 99, 135
OF 36	20		85, 91, 97

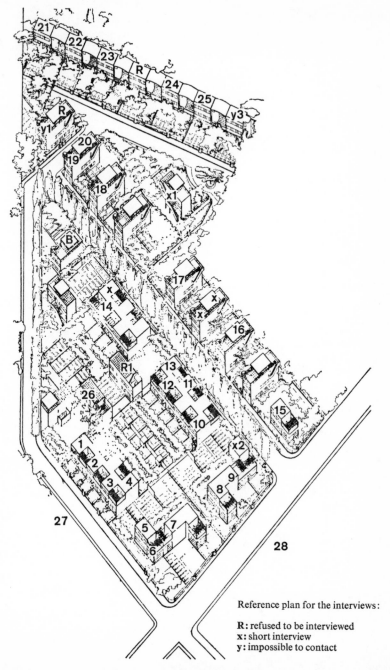

Reference plan for the interviews:

R: refused to be interviewed
x: short interview
y: impossible to contact

61

> 'One could build beautifully
> designed houses, always
> provided the tenant was
> prepared to change his
> outlook.'
> Le Corbusier

5
Group discussion

The failure of Pessac

Five architects with different backgrounds, abilities and interests[1] took part in the group discussion, which lasted for about three hours:

- **B** ... site architect;
- **E** ... structural engineer;
- **G** ... decorator;
- **H** ... architect (prix de Rome);
- **M** ... architect and member of the research group of the Direction de l'Architecture.

There were two principal reasons why I arranged this discussion. In the first place I wanted to gain a deeper insight into Le Corbusier's project and so acquire a better appreciation of its many characteristics; and secondly I wanted to get a group of architects to discuss this architectural project so that I would be able to compare their observations with the remarks made by the occupants in the interviews. I felt that this would enable me to analyse Le Corbusier's original intentions in a more objective way.

It was agreed from the outset that the discussion should be completely open and consequently no attempt was made to impose an agenda. Although quite different from what I had envisaged, the results were

---

[1] The two other members of the group were the sociologist s and the author a.

entirely beneficial, for the fact that the first of my aims was not achieved was highly significant for the second. In fact, nothing that was offered by way of criticism or analysis helped to elucidate the really detailed problems posed by the actual project. All that emerged were *a priori* opinions, which testified on the one hand to a certain knowledge of Le Corbusier and a certain interest in his œuvre, and on the other hand to a certain rigidity of thought on the part of the group members. But, although it was extremely interesting to observe the facility revealed by the group for discussing and elaborating on this architectural project without once feeling the need to visit the actual site – and we shall come to see that this observation bears out one of the conclusions that I have drawn from this study –, it is none the less highly probable that these *a priori* opinions about Le Corbusier's architecture and the intentions underlying it were more informative than any remarks the members of the group might have made on points of detail.

Although the designs were displayed at the beginning of the discussion, although the participants had been sent all the relevant documents in advance and although they had been provided with photographs of the alterations carried out by the occupants (which aroused considerable interest but prompted no detailed comments), the level of analysis was far from sophisticated.

> **G** — I really find this design most interesting.

> **E** — It looks like any other suburb to me, you'll find twenty like it in and around Paris . . .

> **G** — I wish there were twenty like it in the region where I live . . .

What we did hear, however, were general opinions about Pessac which, it need hardly be mentioned, were far more revealing than was apparent to those who expressed them.

> **B** — I think that *the failure of the Pessac project* was due to those difficulties, and our professional attitude is lamentable because we are producing *architecture in which we impose our will on our clients*; we are in a sense *the fascists of the building industry* because we build one cell, then add a second, a third, fourth, fifth, because we impose *predetermined and perfected volumes* reflecting an average sensitivity which, however, never reflects the sensitivity of the people who are going to live [in the houses] . . .

The important point here is not the explanation given for the failure of Pessac but the fact that it was considered to be a failure. This was accepted as self-evident, for nobody ever called the failure of Pessac into question. Le Corbusier seems to have shared this view. That, at least, is the implication of his statement that 'it is always . . . the architect who is wrong'. Moreover, the lady who informed us about this statement also told us: 'Corbu was far too genuine not to have recognized his *mistakes* . . .'

Like the other members of the discussion group, initially I too accepted the failure of Pessac as a self-evident fact. But let us consider another of the explanations given for this failure:

> **E** — That is why the people of Pessac are trying to change
> their houses and make them more personal, because
> there is no possible way in which they can impose their
> will on them . . .

The contradiction in this statement is not immediately apparent and it is hardly surprising that it passed unnoticed at the time. But if we analyse the statement we realize that the people could not have 'changed their houses and made them more personal' unless the architectural design had allowed them sufficient latitude to do so, which means that they were in fact able to 'impose their will on them'. This would, of course, also invalidate the first explanation given for the failure of the project, in which 'architecture in which we impose our will on our clients' came under attack. And if we consider the article by Dr P. Winter, which has been quoted in Chapter 2 and in which the fascist image emerges as a reality, then we find ourselves faced with a dilemma. There can be little doubt about the authoritarian nature of Le Corbusier's architecture: he himself maintained that the tenant must 'change his outlook' whilst Dr Winter spoke of the need – which he doubtless considered to be absolute – for 'changing the life of the modern family in accordance with our precepts'. Moreover, even those members of the group who were favourably disposed towards Le Corbusier, were convinced of his autocratic tendencies:

> **B** — [This was] the attitude of an architect who was very
> sure of his ideas, which he expressed with absolute
> purity of line and by means of harmonies which, in the
> vast majority of cases, we are unable to fault . . .
> [he felt] obliged to impose his will most forcibly in
> expressing an idea . . .

And yet the houses in Pessac lent themselves to conversions and alterations of every kind, a sure sign that the occupants had been allowed a certain degree of liberty.

Le Corbusier as a person

Any interpretation that we may make of the phenomenon of Pessac must inevitably be influenced by our conception of Le Corbusier's personality, which has now been cast in a certain mould, due primarily to the impact of his writings. The plain truth of the matter is that the Pessac project can be regarded either as a success or as a failure on precisely the same grounds. Inevitably, whenever the personality of Le Corbusier was debated, the discussion tended to become polarized. This polarization was established by the two most voluble members of the group, one of whom was for, and the other against, Le Corbusier. The following passages also show the polemical turn taken by the discussion as these two adversaries grew more heated.

> B — Le Corbusier was always creative, and for him to have
> used this type of layout for the Pessac project in the
> hope that others would follow his example – in my
> opinion that shows the attitude of a *pioneer* who was
> genuinely concerned with the problems of living. 1923,
> '24, '25, '26 and '29 – these dates tell us more than
> anything else . . . this was the attitude of a pioneer in
> an era of change . . .

> E — And before then people didn't live? . . .

Here we have on the one hand a value judgement, and on the other sarcasm:

> E — When Muslims go into a mosque they take off their
> shoes, when Catholics go into a church, they dip their
> fingers in holy water, and when we speak of
> architecture we dip our fingers in Le Corbusier . . .
> He is the holy water of architecture . . . I find that just
> as ridiculous as if a doctor who wanted to investigate
> human behaviour were to study frogs or even frog
> spawn and then claim that his findings were universally
> applicable. It is just as ridiculous and just as
> inappropriate. You cannot equate a whole profession –
> a whole area of human activity in which man creates
> his dwelling place, his settlement – with the work of
> just one man, who was born in eighteen . . . something

or other and died in 1965, because this would imply that, before and after him, nothing happened at all. On the contrary, I find that after this 'star performer', this 'Führer', who, having done no more than is set out in the documents that you are holding in your hands – *no more than that, gentlemen* –, discovered how to throw dust in people's eyes by shouting his wares to such an extent architects have come to believe that nothing exists apart from the hogwash served up by his stupid mind . . . As far as I am concerned, this is the basic truth of the matter. And if it is being suggested that Le Corbusier should be considered as the perfect exemplar of twentieth-century architecture, I can only say that I find the suggestion misguided. He was one of those people who are so puffed up with their own deafening publicity that they sweep all before them. And, in point of fact, there were technicians who were more modest than he and techniques which were more valuable than his concrete structures but which have now been completely abandoned: it would be true to say that, both from a technical and moral point of view and in terms of its range, architecture has sunk below its nineteenth-century level; and that is why we do not have enough houses, that is why we do not have enough rooms in the houses that are being built and that is why the people of Pessac are trying to change their houses and make them more personal, because there is no possible way in which they can impose their will on them.

Permutation

A further feature of the discussion was the remarkable way in which the members of the group advanced viewpoints that one would not normally have expected from them. The architect (prix de Rome), for example, was worried about people's *needs:*

> **H** — Our task is to respond to certain needs; *afterwards we can talk about architecture.*

The site architect also appeared to be abandoning his brief:

> **B** — I prefer to speak of *construction* rather than *architecture* . . . *Architecture is a word that frightens me* . . .

architecture cannot be said to exist until the work has been completed: to speak of *producing architecture* is misleading . . .

Meanwhile, the structural engineer, who was concerned in his professional capacity with the investigation of new structures and structural methods, came out in support of decoration, openly accusing Le Corbusier of having suppressed it:

E — I know you sympathize with him, but he was a most inadequate man: by arguing that construction is essentially decorative, although he knew nothing about structural design, and by expressing on his façades a type of construction that was quite worthless, he produced a rather inadequate form of decoration: decoration as we have known it throughout the centuries has disappeared from the façades of our buildings and has been replaced by what is essentially a cliché; you see the inordinate deviationism that has been the hall-mark of this doctrine, which was not really a doctrine at all but which has none the less survived for a long time without being unmasked . . .

At the same time the decorator abjured decoration by invoking Le Corbusier, the great purifier of decorative architecture:

a — You produce decorations, I believe?

G — Yes . . . I don't like the word very much, but I suppose I have to accept some sort of description . . .

E — But you don't like that particular description?

G — I imagine Le Corbusier would have been much more explicit on this point . . . I am in a difficult position because I believe I am doing something that I would not be doing in a normal architectural situation . . . *I would not exist* if we had proper architecture. *There would be no need to add decorations, the architecture would be enough in itself* . . .

Surprisingly, these permutations were remarked upon in the course of the discussion:

E — In antiquity an architect was an entrepreneur and decorator rolled into one; today we have a fluid situation: the modern entrepreneur fulfils a completely new function, the modern architect has become more of a decorator whilst the decorator has been displaced and, since he wishes to retain his place, is at war with the others . . . the situation is confused . . .

Although, strictly speaking, this statement is less than logical, it still draws attention to one of the fundamental problems of the modern period: the fragmentation of architecture as a human activity.

The fact that, in the course of the discussion, various speakers abandoned their own professional viewpoint and advanced arguments that contravened their daily practices would seem to suggest that the members of the group felt the need for a comprehensive form of architecture, in which constructional, decorative, human and economic factors would all combine to provide a single synthetic response.

This was of course precisely what Le Corbusier had tried to achieve at Pessac.

Two special subjects

Quite apart from the fact that it would have been impossible to provide an individual analysis of all the subjects touched upon in the discussion, I felt that it would be preferable and also would make for greater clarity, if the opinions expressed by the group were dealt with in conjunction with similar opinions advanced by the occupants in the course of the interviews. Suffice it to say for the present that most of the subjects broached during the discussion represented different aspects of the antithesis between individual freedom and authoritarianism that has been considered on an earlier page. As far as the members of the group were concerned this antithesis took one of the following forms: movable/fixed, open/closed, complete/incomplete, public/private, collective/individual, juxtaposed/integrated. If we analyse these antithetical forms in slightly greater detail we find that they involve the following factors:

fittings or fixtures,
integrated décor or décor added subsequently,
the state of completion of the houses when they were handed over to the original occupants,
the architectural conception of the houses envisaged as a 'construction game' for the use of the occupants,
the notion of open and closed architecture considered in conjunction

with the fusion between the physical spatial sense and the operative abstract sense, which are derived from the concepts of open and closed states.

These themes, which formed the central core of the discussion, led to the establishment of specific criteria and so provided an interesting comparison with the themes developed by the occupants themselves. Since the group discussion took place before the first series of interviews was conducted it could not have been influenced in any way by remarks made either by the sociologist or myself as a result of our conversations with the occupants. On the other hand, we did not receive the transcript of the discussion until after the initial interviews had been completed; this also precludes any influence in the opposite direction. Consequently, the fact that certain subjects – including those listed above – appeared both in the discussion and in the interviews was all the more significant and was the principal reason why I decided to analyse these two aspects of the enquiry in conjunction with one another.

There are, however, two particular subjects which I now propose to investigate more fully, since they complement the information presented in the first part of this book. But, while I attached considerable importance to these two themes, the members of the group did not. The first, which I have called 'architecture and accommodation' was broached by the sociologist but elicited little response and was discussed for no more than a moment. As for the second, which I have called 'architecture in concrete and military defence', although this prompted one of the members of the group to embark on a lengthy discourse, it did not lead to a general discussion. I, for my part, attached equal importance to both of these themes, for the first illuminates one essential aspect of Le Corbusier's conception whilst the second prompted numerous observations on the part of the occupants, which seem to merit closer consideration.

Architecture and accommodation

I have already drawn attention in a previous chapter to the importance which Le Corbusier attached to the relationship between architecture and accommodation. For him architecture should be rightly 'devoted to dwellings':

> 'It was a pity that modern architecture should have been split into two opposing camps, one of which proclaimed: *first construct,* and the other: *architecture is the skilful, correct and magnificent interplay of volumes assembled in the light.*'

70

This subject was brought up in the course of the discussion by the sociologist but elicited virtually no response:

> S — Is the central problem of architecture and the architect the problem of accommodation? Or is the architect concerned with something different? I don't know, I'm asking you . . .
>
> E — Something different.
>
> B — Of course!

The speakers, the two 'leaders' of the group, were in complete agreement on this point, although in most other respects they had been at loggerheads. On the face of it, one would have been inclined to endorse their view but for the fact that Le Corbusier maintained the exact opposite in so many of his publications. Even the titles of some of his works, such as *La maison des hommes* (The house of men), and, above all, *Une maison, un palais* (A house, a palace), would suggest that he considered architecture and accommodation to be interdependent factors. This would also seem to follow from some of the expressions which he uses. For example, he speaks of 'extensions of dwellings'. To him a church is, above all, just such an extension, and he once declined a commission to build a church because it failed to fulfil this purpose:

> 'My job is to *house people*, to provide them with a concrete container which will enable them to lead a more human life. How could I build a church for people whom I had not housed? One day perhaps I will be asked to build a church for a *cité d'habitation;* that I would find meaningful . . .'

Considered in this wider sense, the major part of Le Corbusier's œuvre was in fact concerned with accommodation: in addition to numerous projects for dwellings, villas, *unités d'habitation* and so on he also built churches, stadia and youth hostels . . . And for him a monastery was, first and foremost, a dwelling place.

Thus, we find the two group leaders flatly denying the existence of any connexion between architecture and accommodation whilst Le Corbusier quite evidently regarded them as interdependent, which means that this is still very much an open question.

That Le Corbusier really did try to 'produce architecture' at Pessac is undeniable. That the concepts of *architecture* and *accommodation* are capable of the kind of fusion he envisaged is not.

E — (*In the nineteenth century*) . . . there was a wide range
of techniques. Industrialized building was far more
advanced then than it is today: stanchions, small
tee-beams and prefabricated ceiling sections were being
produced and could be bought all along the Porte des
Lilas; there were places where you could even buy a
whole prefabricated house, which could be erected in
a matter of weeks. In Paris and in the major countries
of the West you still find clear traces of this kind of
architecture (*metal architecture*), for example the
'galeries' or 'passages' of Paris with their lightweight
arcades. But this lightweight architecture has been
abandoned. Why? I imagine it was due to the
development of aviation, because there was a constant
threat of war and people felt insecure when they found
themselves in what were virtually cold frames. And so,
once aeroplanes were used for bombing raids, it was
decided – and these were legal measures, mark you –
that all such structures must be covered by a concrete
roof at least thirty and, in certain countries, sometimes
fifty centimetres thick. The growing number of such
concrete roofs made people feel more secure. And then,
of course, a few idiots began to shout: 'it's art! it's
art!', whereas in actual fact it was simply an anti-
aircraft measure. In order to build the Maginot Line
they had to start producing cement on an unbelievable
and unprecedented scale . . . unfortunately for the
cement industry we don't always have wars; sometimes
we have peace. There are interludes, and during the
interludes these industries had to be kept on full
production, some means had to be found of disposing
of their product, which is essentially spurious because
it is heavy, difficult to handle and creates echoes; we
know the sort of problems it poses, we know people
who are driven mad by the sound of voices from the
floor above. Moreover, this material is thermoductile,
which creates heating problems. Finally, it is a material
which – as every schoolboy knows – is unsuitable for
the supposedly revolutionary purposes for which M.
Le Corbusier proposed to use it. So there you are!
You now have a reasonably accurate account of the
technical revolution that you have believed in for the
past twenty years.

But this account was none too well received by the other members of the group, who thought it biased:

> **B** — You speak of bombing raids. But, unless I have been misinformed, there was no question of such raids prior to the '14–'18 war; and M. Perret was using reinforced concrete long before 1914 and, it so happens, produced a number of extremely interesting works; and before him there was M. Hennebique . . .

> **G** — Of course, Perret! everyone knows about Perret. It's common knowledge. So I really can't accept your argument . . .

In Chapter 1 I referred to the article by Le Corbusier which had persuaded Frugès to commission him for the Pessac project and in which Le Corbusier mentioned the possibility of using building techniques originally evolved for military purposes. This military facet of Le Corbusier's architecture is not unimportant for our appreciation of his Pessac design and, as it happens, one of the interviewees made some highly significant observations in this connexion. The man in question was the only person who had gone to live in Pessac *on account of* Le Corbusier, for whose work he had a veritable passion. Because of this, his assessments of the aesthetic quality of Le Corbusier's buildings were particularly interesting. In one of his comments, which was prompted by the *unités d'habitation* in Marseille he referred specifically to the *Blockhaus* quality of his architecture:

> **M 22** — What I like enormously about Marseille is the stilts; the stilts in Marseille are so . . . *well, so squat*!

> **a** — And . . . that's what makes them attractive . . . the fact that they're squat . . .

> — Yes! Now . . . I'd like to mention something entirely personal. As you have seen, I am interested in the history of military equipment[2] and, you know . . . I have a certain liking for . . . or rather . . . I take an interest in *Blockhäuser* . . . but . . . not . . . as military installations, rather as . . . plastic objects. You see, I am also very much taken with Ledoux's buildings . . . I suppose that corresponds to . . . well, I don't rightly

---

[2] This man actually collected small models of chariots and other military equipment.

know, it would take a psychoanalyst to say what it corresponds to . . . but in the stilts of Marseille and in quite a few other places as well, in his unfinished concrete which shows the marks of the shuttering, you find the kind of force which . . . which interests me in the *Blockhäuser* . . .

It would be a mistake to regard this as an isolated reaction. This particular trend of modern architecture is still very much alive and Le Corbusier's unfinished concrete, which reproduces the grain of the timber used for the shuttering, is still a common feature of present-day buildings. The church designed by Claude Parent and Paul Virilio in Nevers, which was directly inspired by *Blockhaus* architecture, is a particularly striking example.[3]

Incidentally, the '*Blockhaus* quality' of Le Corbusier's work was also mentioned in another interview, where, however, it was assessed in pejorative terms:

M 19 — It's a bit like a *Blockhaus*.

It is interesting to note that this person also spoke unfavourably of concrete as a building material:

M 19 — Amongst modern materials I like glass, metal, steel, aluminium; I don't like concrete . . .

This interviewee was like **E** in so far as he connected the use of reinforced concrete with a certain type of architecture of military origin. But, in addition to this association, we also found that concrete was linked with security and war.

M 2 — You want to know how strong these houses are: that house over there was blasted by a bomb; the terrace fell to the ground but wasn't demolished and the staircase remained standing. I tell you . . . huh! *you want to know if it's strong* . . . I'll say it's strong . . . and, you know, I wanted to cut into the walls . . . well, I tell you . . . I came across iron bars . . . lots of them . . . and when they say it's reinforced concrete, well . . . take it from me, it's reinforced all right . . . before that falls down, huh, when all the other houses have fallen down mine will still be standing, that's for sure!

[3] For a comparison between the Church of St Bernadette in Nevers and various *Blockhäuser* see C. PARENT and P. VIRILIO, *Architecture–Principe*, No.7. With their review the authors provide a number of impressive photographs.

The association between reinforced concrete and security is quite obvious in this interview. So too is the association with strength. In this respect concrete appears as the direct antithesis of metal, and when we come to investigate the 'construction game' we will see that this gives rise to a further antithesis between strength and mobility.

'Even if it were true that
the notions of universality
and totality, of the total
man, and of interaction
within this totality, are not
unproblematical, this would
not be a sufficient reason
for discarding them . . .'
H. Lefèbvre

6
The interviews: the parts of the house and the house as an entity

In this chapter I propose to reproduce one of the shorter interviews virtually verbatim. But, although comparatively short, this interview none the less conveys a definite impression of the profound resonance which life, in all its fullness, is able to produce in a dwelling house. In fact, its very brevity enables it to do this all the more effectively. This interview shows how a house, despite its apparent passivity and the vicissitudes to which it may be subject, can provide a perfect target for the projection of a wide range of feelings and faithfully reflects the image that people form of themselves at certain moments in their lives. A house expresses the universality of life. For this reason, I felt that I should reproduce one of the interviews at length since it is only in its totality that an interview can represent the totality of 'living'.

a — So you think it's badly done.

M 14 — Yes, **very badly done,** I'd say . . . that, for example, over there, he could have done better than that . . . look here . . . look, the rain gets in everywhere . . . here, I did that [*roofed over the patio*] I did it, but you know, the bombardments, you know what they do . . . they thought they were performing miracles. Well, believe me . . . I've worked a bit on buildings in my time, and you know . . . **I've seen quite different things, you know! oh yes!** . . . I have a room here, it has a gaping ceiling . . . and then there are the gutters, but he [*the owner*] never attends to them . . . all he does is raise the rent, but he never does any repairs . . . it's getting on for twelve thousand and something . . . so of course . . .

a — You might have bought it earlier on?

— Well yes, because then, we would have redone the walls . . . we would have refaced the inside walls with bricks . . . but *now* . . . the oldest boy has had a house built for himself . . . the second has had an accident, he walks on crutches . . . the third has also left, to join his regiment . . . although he's just had an accident as well . . . but you can't live like that . . . no . . . a different sort of house, certainly, because that might have . . . look: what is all that supposed to mean? . . . you'd think you were in . . . it's the sort of thing the Marabouts would have over in Africa . . . look, over there, the pergolas . . . what use are they? . . . it would have been better to have fixed up a couple of extra rooms in a hut . . . rather than have that thing hanging up there [*the terrace*], and you know, it's all going to chip away in the course of time . . . the cement will die . . . the old iron will make it crack and then where are you . . . *buy that* . . . I ask you . . . buy that! But they should take that away [*the terrace*] . . . and you wouldn't want to be on your own when you were taking it away! . . . those things are heavy . . . there are iron bars in there as thick as that. So, although Le Corbusier should have been able to put up a tall building, you know, with all that iron . . . when you stand and look at them . . . not even a pig would want to go in . . . you go and look at one *now*! it [*one of Le Corbusier's 'skyscrapers'*[1]] is worth at least thirteen million . . . *now* I just can't keep the water out . . . it would be decent otherwise . . . You know, we used to eat there before [*on the patio*] . . . with the children . . . *now* we always eat in the house . . .

a — It was better before . . .

— Hm . . . well, you know, then it was in the open . . .

---

[1] The three-storeyed villas in Pessac were referred to locally as 'skyscrapers'.

now I've done that [*roofed in the patio*] and the rain still gets in . . . when they start their bombardment [*a reference to sonic booms from jet aircraft*]*:* the door flies open, the dog bolts for his life . . . when they explode their damned bombs . . . because they're beginning to get at us too . . . the sick people over there: d'you think that does them any good? . . . we had a nice, quiet place here before . . . *now,* since they've been building houses . . . look, *now* it's a proper town they've built over there . . . my wife was in tears . . . she didn't want to stop here . . . and it was all quiet before . . . now the children are getting married . . . I'm not asking for a mansion . . . but I would like to be under a roof . . . my neighbours have all bought their houses . . . the whole block . . . I'm the only one who hasn't bought his house . . .

a — But there are other tenants . . .

— You think so! . . . I'm the only one . . . they've all bought . . . there's only me is a tenant . . . Look! . . . the cat . . . now, he really is something special . . .

a — You have other animals?

— Yes . . . another cat and a dog . . .

Apart from a few words of introduction and farewell this constituted virtually the whole of the interview.

The first thing that strikes us in this extract is the syntax, which expresses the close involvement between living in a house and living as such: 'the third has also left, to join his regiment . . . although he's just had an accident as well . . . but you can't live like that . . . no . . . a different sort of house, certainly, because that might have . . .'

I have drawn attention to the repetition of the word 'now' by printing it in italics. By insisting on this comparison between past and present the tenant would seem to imply that the house was no longer the same as it had once been. It will have aged, of course. But which changed first: the tenant's life or his house? Or – bearing in mind their close involvement – should we conclude that they aged together?

We see, therefore, that it is difficult to separate the concept of 'living in a house' from the other aspects of living. If further proof of the universality of this concept is required, we need only consider the impasse that would soon be reached if we were to analyse, point by point, the various individual parts that go to make up a house. Take, for example, Le Corbusier's wide windows. These, which were one of the key points of the modern style of architecture evolved by Le Corbusier, were modified by many of the occupants and constituted one of the most striking aspects of the alterations observed in Pessac. The occupants apparently preferred the traditional types of window, whose validity Le Corbusier called into question in his 'Conversation with Students from the Schools of Architecture':

> 'How do you make a window? But *à propos:* what is the function of a window? do you really know why we make windows? If you know, tell me. If you know, you will be able to explain to me why we make square windows, arched windows, rectangular windows and so on . . . I want to know the reason why. But first and foremost: do we need windows today?'

After first calling into question the efficacy of windows as such Le Corbusier finally opted for the 'wide window'. Thanks to the new structural developments which had taken place the façades of houses no longer had to be loadbearing, which meant that windows could be built across their entire width.

> 'The *wide window* is, in fact, a *glass section* that we have incorporated into something that has nothing to do with the past.'

In the Q.M.F. more than half of the original 'wide windows' have been made narrower. The reasons given for this particular conversion were many and varied:

F 13 — We asked him [*the owner*] for narrower windows so as to have more . . .

a — You don't like large apertures . . .

— No, I do not, I've had them: in the first place, they're very awkward, you have to sit on the sill to clean the glass . . . and when you're on the first floor, you know . . . And then the metal frames lose their shape . . . now the frame has been remade in wood, it's fine . . .

F 6 — . . . During the war, with all the bombing, the window
panes were blown out; in those days you just couldn't
get large sheets of glass, so people had to make their
windows smaller.

F 3 — . . . When the windows were the full width of the house
the youngsters next door used to amuse themselves by
teasing the children we had here . . . so we blocked
the window off . . . and then we put this single window
in the centre, I prefer it like that . . .

OF 35 — The windows aren't very pretty, are they?

a — Why not?

— Why not? . . . well, because they're ugly.

a — . . .

— What I find so ugly about these windows is the metal
uprights, you see, there are too many of them. A
window like this should either be completely blank or
else it should have little square panes . . .

In their explanations the occupants advanced functional, rational and
aesthetic reasons for having changed the original windows. But, although they always had some such argument ready to hand, in actual
fact they were often motivated by quite different considerations, which
were based on established standards of taste. The occupant who said
that he 'preferred' his modified window to the original was clearly basing his assessment on traditional criteria whilst the final excerpt cited
above, in which the occupant insisted that large windows should either
be completely blank or else should have little square panes, provides a
perfect illustration of conservative thinking.

This conservatism was also demonstrated by a contradiction that
occurred in another interview, in which a lady informed us that she
always kept her shutters closed because, with its great expanse of glass,
the wide window let in too much heat in the summer, so much so that
her curtains were scorched by the sun, whilst in the winter the same
window caused a loss of heat. Later, this lady told us that in another
room, which faced in exactly the same direction as the first, she was
thinking of having a large bay built on overlooking the garden 'as is
customary nowadays' so as to create more living space. But the only
difference between a 'wide window' and a 'large bay' would seem to be

that one is 'customary' and the other is not, which would suggest that in this particular case conservatism had developed into conformism.

But wouldn't there be better things to look for than explanations of individual features? And even assuming that the real reason why the occupants reduced the width of their windows was their inherent conformism, we still have to account for this conformism . . .

The difficulties posed by this method of procedure, whereby the occupants' reactions to specific parts of their houses are treated in isolation, are seen in a new light when we consider their attitudes to the terraces, although to be precise we ought really to speak of 'roof terraces' or 'roof gardens'. Like the wide windows these constitute an important feature of Le Corbusier's architectural conception and so call for individual investigation despite the problematical nature of this method:

> 'The roof garden is a new device which can be put to
> agreeable uses . . . reinforced concrete provides the
> support for the roof terrace and for the 15 or 20 cm
> of earth which makes up the *roof garden*.'

What did the occupants have to say about this feature of their houses?

> **a** — Do you go up on to the terrace?

> **F 1** — Oh no, not for any length of time . . . it's hot up there
> . . . and then, you know, when there's a wind like
> today, it's cold.

> **M 13** — It's my parents who have that room . . . but if it was
> me, I'd use it, you could make a summer garden on
> the terrace which would be very modern . . .

> **a** — Do you go on the terrace?

> **M 9** — Oh yes . . . now it's . . . we used to be able to eat up
> there, we used to eat there . . .

> **F 13** — The terrace, like the verandah, serves no practical
> purpose, so we've gradually come to use it for storage,
> we put out . . . things, old things, old furniture . . . not
> big things, of course . . . they could have made an
> extra room out of it with an entrance door, that would
> have provided additional space . . .

The quotation on pp. 55–56 (**F 6**) might also have been profitably inserted here. But the following passage covers literally every aspect of this complex issue:

> **F 15** — . . . the terrace is very big! yes, yes indeed, a very large area! but why didn't they think of providing an outside staircase: to get there you have to . . . come up these stairs . . . and then pass through a room that was designed as a bedroom . . . A terrace is always decked out with flowers of some sort, and that entails a lot of toing and froing with water and earth . . . What about the poor housewife? Anyway, look here . . . you know, it's almost a joke . . . nobody ever uses these terraces, except for the big buildings over there on the right, where the people use their big flat terrace, which is right at the top of the house, to hang out their washing . . . but nobody arranges flower-beds or puts out wrought iron tables and chairs like the people in Arago or Camponnac. And why? because they have loggias [*in Arago*] with direct access from the living room. So you can go straight from the living room to the terrace without having to pass through a bedroom on the way. True, in the modern high-rise buildings they've also built loggias with access from the bedroom. *But you know, it's . . . it's different . . .* the loggia goes with the room, so nobody is inconvenienced . . .

What are we to conclude from these extracts? That it is hot on the terraces but that they could be turned into summer gardens . . . that people don't go on them now although they used to once . . . that the terraces as such are fine but that the type of access is open to criticism (even though access to the loggias in modern high rise buildings is also from the bedrooms, because there 'it's different') . . . What we have, in effect, is a series of contradictory statements. Considered individually they may seem perfectly reasonable, but clearly they cannot be regarded as constituting irrefutable criticisms.

I therefore decided that I would have to disregard the apparently objective criticisms of points of detail formulated by the occupants and concentrate instead on their impressions, which are far more interesting. The oriental character of the houses, which we shall be analysing later and which was alluded to by many of the occupants, was closely linked with the terraces:

> **OF 35** — This patio, these terraces, that all makes for a lot of
> wasted space in our wet climate . . .

This is an impression and not a criticism, since the speaker did not live
in the Q.M.F. and had never visited any of the houses there. Clearly, the
space occupied by the terraces could only be said to have been wasted
if there was a lack of space in the houses as a whole. In point of fact,
however, these houses were reasonably spacious. One inclines to the
view, therefore, that this statement – 'that all makes for a lot of wasted
space' – is of the same order as a later statement made by the same interviewee – 'that makes a somewhat oriental impression'. We touch here
upon the problem posed by the distinction between actions and words,
between the sensible level and the verbal level, between what a thing
'makes for' or 'makes' and what it 'is'. Nothing demonstrates this distinction more clearly than the sort of discrepancies between words and
actions that we were able to observe in Pessac. After assuring us that he
made good use of his terrace – eating there in the summer and, as is the
custom in Bordeaux, even sleeping there on very hot nights – and after
proudly showing us that it was possible to discern from his terrace the
outline of the new bridge in Bordeaux, one of our interviewees blandly
went on to regret the fact that he had not been rich enough to buy a
house with a proper roof. A second interviewee, who went on his terrace
just once a year to effect any necessary repairs, told us that he was very
glad to be able to go up on the roof whenever he felt like it:

> **M 3** — Here there is even a terrace . . . I can even take my
> ease on the roof . . . you think that isn't pleasant? . . .

Here, surely, we have the two component aspects of the image which
embraces the totality of a house: on the one hand the traditional roof
and on the other the roof that you can walk on, the 'roof garden', of
which Le Corbusier said that it provided 'a pleasure that was once
enjoyed by certain civilizations'. Is it surprising, therefore, that the
residents of Pessac should have regarded these terraces as the really
distinctive feature of their houses?

> **OF 35** — The really surprising feature is the terraces . . . they
> make a somewhat oriental impression . . .

Subsequently, the same person told us:

> **OF 35** — Taken all in all . . . the sort of style I like, you know,
> is . . . a big house with a big roof.

Roof or terrace, a house is a *single* structure that is surmounted by a sign.

> M 7 — If I change the style of the roof . . . the design being what it is, essentially square, if you put a roof on top you destroy the whole character of the house.

But there are two sorts of signs: object signs and word signs. At the object level a roof is something material, something physical. A terrace, on the other hand, is not material, it is a plane or, at most, an architectural abstraction . . . in the final analysis it is simply the absence of a roof, as is indicated by the following extract:

> OF 36 — It was surprising, after the traditional lean-to houses, to see these terraced roofs . . . *these houses have no roofs* . . .

The reader will no doubt have noticed that, before describing a 'terrace' as a simple structure, I first had to enlarge on this concept by defining it as a 'roof terrace' or 'roof garden'. In fact, these expressions were furnished by Le Corbusier himself.

Amongst the general public such expressions still persist: in referring to his terrace one of the occupants constantly spoke of his roof notwithstanding the fact that a terrace makes a strange sort of roof. The truth of the matter is that this particular occupant found himself in an unknown world; he had even lost all sense of certain basic facts such as the weight of water and the rate at which it evaporates . . .

> M 15 — The roof, I don't know . . . I've never been up there . . . there are cracks on the underside . . . up on the roof it must be a regular watershed . . . I don't know . . . I've never been up there . . . I don't know whether they've provided a gully – normally they'd have to provide one . . . or whether they expect the water to evaporate . . .

In this extract the repetition of the word 'roof' – which evokes a concept and an object both of which are well known – and the strange, indefinable quality of the object under discussion – the terrace – are perfect foils . . .

Houses are synthetic structures made up of many different components and amongst those components there are some which make for universality.

'We-all-of-us-always-have-
our-own-ideas! We want
our own house—don't we!
—for ourselves. . . . and
we want it the way . . .
the way we want to have it'
M. L. (Pessac resident).

7
The interviews:
the occupants' conceptions

We have seen that, although a house is a corporate entity that cannot
easily be reduced to its component parts, some of those components –
the roof or the terrace, for example – help to emphasize its universality.
However, a house can also be regarded in other ways, depending on the
outlook of the person concerned. And in this connexion some of the
conceptions advanced by the Pessac residents seemed to me to be sufficiently interesting to merit inclusion here.

Initial impressions: strange and alien

Most of the passages quoted in this section are taken from interviews
with people who moved to Pessac when the houses were first built
between 1926 and 1930. We have already seen that these original occupants were far from happy about their new homes and that their anxiety
was greatly increased by the bad name given to the district, which had
been virtually declared taboo by the local residents.

> **F 6** — At first, you know, very few people ever came here,
> you know, to this neck of the woods . . .

> **M 3** — At first there were some queer people here . . . things
> had been badly arranged . . . because there was that
> new law passed by Minister Loucheur . . . nobody
> paid . . . that put a lot of people off . . . at first, we
> weren't accustomed to square houses, and then there

87

was the colour . . . it wasn't very nice, that maroon.
No, it wasn't nice . . . not nice at all, it made . . . that
put a lot of people off too, that colour . . . They
didn't say to themselves: 'Oh well, we can always
repaint it.'

F 3 — We were outcasts . . . – What! You live in the
Moroccan district? . . . – And so I said to myself:
'Well, that's lovely! and what if I don't like it? What
am I going to do? . . .' It was terrible . . . I felt as if
I was going to prison. I asked before we bought the
house whether, if we didn't like it, we would be able
to resell. I was told we would . . . so, that was all
right . . . But when I told people we were going to
buy a house there: – What! you're moving to that
district! Oh, it's no good there! – So I said: 'If we're
not going to find a buyer, should we go ahead? . . .'
But nine out of every ten who told me it was 'no good'
hadn't even set foot in the district. They hadn't even
seen it.

a — You had to overcome [these prejudices] . . .

— Well, yes. So I said: 'If I don't like it there . . . what
are we going to do? . . . I'd been influenced a bit by
this . . . assessment; and then, once we'd moved in,
we liked it . . . and we stayed; and we will stay . . .
Now, I said: 'It's a bit big for us, but anyway . . . we're
all right here.'

Initially, many of the interviewees were unable to give adequate reasons
for their feelings of aversion:

F 6 — At first my husband didn't like it here, he didn't like
it at all.

a — What was it that he didn't like?

— He didn't like **anything** . . . he took it . . . you know
. . . I had to **force** him to agree, but he **did-not-like-it!**
And then, afterwards, he got used to it, and he told
me: – Buying this house turned out to be a good idea,

after all. – We got used to it and then **we liked it, we liked it very much.**

a — Was it the style of the house that he didn't like?

— Phew . . . I don't know . . . you know . . . when you're dead set against a thing, hm, you don't really know why. I don't know . . . He never told me what it was he didn't like. The district perhaps? Or the house? But whatever it was . . . he didn't like it, he didn't like it at all . . .   . . .

Finally, she furnished explanations:

F 6 — It was more than modern . . . I believe it was Le Corbusier's first project, and . . . you know, people didn't like it . . . They didn't like the style . . . no . . . hm . . . they called it the Moroccan district. Yes, because they said the houses were Moroccan, they were built in the Moroccan style; but we . . . from the outside . . . (my husband was in the colonies) from the outside I didn't like it very much, and then, once I had looked over the house, really, I was completely won over by the design, by the layout of the rooms, which were large, very bright, very airy and well aligned, and as for the outside, well, you know, we had it repainted, had it done up, it really was very good . . . hm . . . you know, it was the prettiest house in the district in '42 . . .

Again and again we find this evocation of North African architecture. However, it is only the *outsides* of the houses – and, more especially, the terraces – that are involved in this comparison.

M 3 — It looked Algerian, it was a colonial style.

a — What made you think that?

— Well, in the first place, those houses with their terraces and their square . . . cubist shapes, and then . . . that terrace style. And down below there were the patios, you know . . .

In other words, the evocation of Arab architecture was prompted, firstly, by the terraces and, secondly, by the terraces . . .

> **M 14** — [*pointing at the terrace*] Look! What is the point of that? . . . you'd think you were . . . amongst the Marabouts, over there, in Africa . . .

This statement goes to the heart of the matter: the occupants found the terraces quite meaningless and, since it was imperative that they should have a meaning, they made this comparison with Arab architecture. For them objects could not exist in their own right, they had to evoke other objects and so enter into a meaningful context. The important thing about this evocation of Arab architecture on the part of the occupants of the Q.M.F. was their apparent need to identify with a specific country or specific region a type of architecture which they insisted on regarding as alien because they found it strange. It would, of course, be quite a simple matter to find alternative meanings for Le Corbusier's architecture. The description of the Pessac houses, quoted on an earlier page, as 'Frugès cubes of sugar' was, in fact, an attempt to do precisely that. But the most significant point in this connexion, one that needs to be emphasized, is the fact that Le Corbusier's Pessac houses, which were executed in an 'international' as opposed to a 'regional' style, were quite literally 'regionalized' by their occupants and, more especially, by local observers.

> **OF 35** — It seems that this architecture has not been integrated, that it is out of place . . . It is the sort of architecture I would like to see in a tropical country . . . One surprising feature is the use of terraces . . . they look rather . . . rather oriental, those terraces . . .

The lady who made this statement (and who does not live in the Q.M.F.) might perhaps have been expected to provide a fairly precise definition of what constitutes local, regional or national architecture. In fact, she was rather vague on this point:

> — To my mind, the sort of building that would suit **this place** would be a big house with a four-sided pitched roof.

The regional stereotype: the 'lean-to house'

None the less, there is such a thing as regional architecture. We have already encountered it in Chapter 1, where we considered the significance of the 'lean-to house' and the 'country house'. In the interviews these traditional buildings were defined in two ways:

Externally:
> **OF 36** — A lean-to house is a long, low, symmetrical building situated at the side of the road ... whereas a country house is set back from the road; there are also other obvious differences between a lean-to house and a country house.

Internally:
> **OF 32** — The lean-to house has ... a central corridor with rooms on either side and a verandah at the back, that is the Bordeaux style, you know ... I would have liked one myself ... If I had had the means ...

In fact, many of the interviewees tended to regard this type of structure as ideal:

> **OF 33** — There's only one bad thing about these houses: you have to pass through the living room to enter the other rooms ... my parents always had a lean-to house ... perhaps that's why I would like a central corridor ...

This last person is now living in a house which was built in 1960 in another settlement[1] but which has precisely the same interior layout as the houses in Pessac: the front door opens into the living room.

But I must define the lean-to house a little more exactly. There are two basic types: a 'double-fronted' house, which is the type described above (**F 32**), and a 'single-fronted' house, which is normally semi-detached with a corridor running alongside the party wall and giving access to rooms on one side only. Le Corbusier's design lent itself quite readily to simple alterations, which allowed the Pessac houses to be brought more or less into line with the traditional lean-to house. By erecting a partition wall the occupants could – and in many cases did – build a corridor running along one side of their houses, thus creating the really essential feature of the single-fronted lean-to house. One of the residents, who was not a native of the Bordeaux region, commented on this type of structure:

[1] See Chapter 4, p.56.

M 3 — You know, here, when I come into the house, I really feel that I've come home . . . it's not bad, is it . . . it's normal.

s — Normal . . .

— Yes, although . . . you would never think so from the outside . . . I tell you, that's why some people didn't want to come here . . . but here . . . me . . . I'm at home! After all, I have a dining-room, I have a kitchen . . . I have . . . a little parlour, a studio, bedrooms. Well, that's good enough for me, I've got everything I need . . . Lots of them put up a partition, along there, so as not to have to say 'We walk straight into the living room' . . . no, they didn't like that . . . They had to have the sort of entrance they had in their old houses, over there . . . in the town, you know . . . lean-to houses they're called in Bordeaux: they always have an entrance corridor. Well! They all came from lean-to houses, so they wanted to walk into a corridor and not straight into the living room.

In other words, for the people of the Bordeaux region a 'normal' house was a lean-to house[2] whilst for this particular interviewee the new houses in Pessac were 'normal', although in order to convince himself that they were normal he felt obliged to point out that they contained all the usual offices . . . dining-room, kitchen, bedrooms, etc., which would suggest that he did not really consider them normal at all, certainly 'you would never think so from the outside'. In fact, it is questionable whether this particular interviewee had any definite conception of what constituted a normal house. But then, what people actually mean when they use this expression is no doubt simply that they have come to accept that there are such things as normal houses, to which they are prepared to adapt since they have no option anyway . . .

M 3 — We live like kings here . . . What more can you ask? . . .

s — Everybody has his own ideas about his house . . .

[2] The first of the three designs reproduced at the end of the illustration section (pp. 196–198) illustrates the kind of influence exerted by the traditional lean-to house. This design was made by a boy of about 10 years of age, who lives in a modern house with an open-plan interior built by his father, who is an architect. Although the boy had no corridor in his own home, he none the less incorporated a corridor into his design.

— Oh, indeed they do, indeed they do. There's no doubt about that. Take me, before I came to live here, I always had the idea, I had a house . . . a house in my mind . . . I had it all planned, you understand. I knew that if one day I was to build a house for myself: it was all there, the whole layout, you know. Well, there it was . . . And now, if that were to happen now, if I were to build a house for myself . . . well then, I would have my own ideas: that's what I want . . .

s — What would the house be like? . . .

— Oh . . . You know, now, with the cars and all that, now, I don't think about it much . . . What I'm saying is *if* I were to do it, I would have my own ideas; now . . . after all the things I've seen, I might make certain modifications, but basically . . . **We-all-of-us-always-have-our-own-ideas! We want our own house, don't we! for ourselves . . . and we want it the way . . . the way we want to have it!**[3]

External and internal qualities

At the beginning of the previous section I quoted two definitions of the lean-to house. The first of these (**F 35**), which dealt with the external appearance of such houses, was given by a lady who was not particularly interested in this type of architecture. She now lives in a house with a garden and her ideal home would be a country house set in its own grounds. The second definition (**F 33**), which was concerned with the interior layout, came from a person who was clearly very much involved with the lean-to house (My parents always had a lean-to house . . . perhaps that is why I would like a central corridor) . . . The different attitudes of these two people – one objective and disinterested, the other committed and peremptory – are reflected in their choice of language. Thus, the first, who described the exterior, spoke of '*a* lean-to house' whilst the second, who was concerned with the interior, spoke of '*the* lean-to house'. Perhaps I am attaching too much significance to what could conceivably be a purely fortuitous distinction. But, on the other hand, it was noticeable that the interviewees tended to form widely differing assessments of the external and internal qualities of the villas:

[3] The house occupied by this interviewee has been reproduced in illustration 70.

F 3 — . . . nine out of every ten who told me it was 'no good' hadn't even set foot in the district . . .

and the wife of this interviewee continued:

— I'd been influenced a bit by this . . . assessment; and then, once we'd moved in . . .

F 6 — From the outside I didn't like it very much, and then, once I had looked over the house, really, I was completely won over . . .

M 3 — When I come into the house, I really feel that I've come home . . . it's not bad, is it! . . . it's normal . . . although . . . you would never think so from the outside . . .

In general, people preferred the interiors to the exteriors:

F 3 — Visitors tend to say: I would never have believed that the interior was so pleasant. With that staircase you could imagine yourself on board a ship. Very nice! – But the outside is not so good.

M 2 — As for the outside . . . Believe me, people were quite put out by this kind of structure . . . It didn't bother me, but . . . once we went into the house we were **astounded** by the modern conveniences that we saw . . . At that time, 1930, virtually the only houses to have such amenities were those built for middle-class people . . .

But there was one exception to this general rule:

— The interior is not at all what one expects. The exterior and interior don't harmonize. From the outside the houses look very impressive, especially this type. But as far as the interior is concerned, they are not ideal to live in. (I am not speaking for my husband as well) . . .

After enumerating the various interior conversions that might profitably be undertaken the interviewee continued:

— And then, once all that had been done, I think *the exterior would begin to look like the interior* . . .

94

But this lady, whose view of the houses was diametrically opposed to that of the *majority group*, adopted a completely different attitude when asked to comment on the *district*:

> **F 15** — A lot of people, when they first see this district, are
> horrified . . . *that's the impression it makes at first sight*:
> it is fearful . . . *those walls painted all the colours of the*
> *rainbow*, to be perfectly honest, it is very ugly, *but then* . . .
> *when you live here*, as I was telling you, you are able to
> maintain a certain privacy, people don't spy on you,
> they don't see everything you do because the houses are
> isolated even though they are terraced: one garden is in
> front of the house, the next at the back . . .

Having proceeded from an assessment of the interior qualities of the houses to an appreciation of their exterior qualities the next logical step would be to make the transition from architecture to town planning by considering the entire district as opposed to considering individual houses. And, in fact, we shall be reporting the observations made by the occupants concerning the district as a whole and evaluating their attitudes to their environment later on. Meanwhile, however, it might be profitable to establish a parallel between the two parts of the interview quoted above (**F 15**), the first of which was concerned with the house, the second with the district.

In both cases we find:

(1) Firstly, an exterior aspect which is either 'impressive' or 'not impressive' and which reflects an artificial assessment in both a literal and a figurative sense.

(2) And, secondly, a long-term assessment of life both in the district and in the houses: 'When you live here', 'they [the houses] are/are not ideal to live in.'

Some occupants, of course, were only able to assess the external quality of the houses or the district, this being their only concern:

> **M 17** — When you go somewhere new, if there is anything bad,
> you notice it at once . . . the very first day . . . afterwards,
> when you get used to it, you pay no attention. Things
> you fail to see on the first day are lost for ever, you just
> don't see them any more . . .

> **OF 35** — I cannot give an opinion, I don't live there.

Invariably the aesthetic judgement of the occupants was brought to bear on the external appearance of the houses:

> **M 20** — From an aesthetic point of view . . . I didn't like it,
> especially the outside . . . but I saw its potential
> immediately . . .

We also find different values being placed on the district, depending on whether it is considered as an architectural or a sociological cluster:

> **M 19** — As far as external appearances are concerned the district
> is a slum area . . . but from a sociological point of view
> it is far from being a slum area.

In the light of this observation it is somewhat surprising to find that a social worker was primarily concerned with the aesthetic aspect of the villas:

> **F 20** — If they were classified as 'historic monuments' I'd never
> stop laughing . . . to my mind historic monuments are . . .
> on the one hand more ancient . . . and on the other hand
> more aesthetic . . . it would be an insult to Versailles . . .
> *it is not presentable* . . . .

However, this social worker did recognize certain sociologically desirable features, although she failed to give Le Corbusier any credit for them:

> — You know, there is no friction here . . . the families are
> juxtaposed, not superimposed (*the social worker lives in
> a semidetached house*) . . . as a social worker I know
> only too well what goes on in big blocks like those over
> there (*high rise buildings a hundred metres long and twelve
> storeys high; see illustration 41*), one troublemaker in a
> building of that sort can poison a whole staircase, from
> that point of view we are well off here . . . but frankly . . .
> tell me frankly, do you like these houses? . . .

The architect's conception

This last quotation raises the question of the architect's conception Clearly, in the opinion of this interviewee historic monuments are places like Versailles, for her Architecture is spelled with a capital A, and it is only at this exalted level that she is prepared to concede any effective role to the architect. The fact that life in the district was pleasant apparently had nothing to do with Le Corbusier; it just happened to be that way. Her attitude to the house in which she lived was essentially the same:

F 20 — I realize that he let light into his houses . . . . .

This empty cliché, which she had picked up at second hand, shows just how impersonal her judgement was.

It was widely believed by the occupants that the architect's real role was essentially aesthetic and was concerned primarily with questions of style. It was not what he did but the way that he did it that was important. Because, come what may, the one thing that an architect was bound to do was to follow the instructions of his client, who assumed full responsibility for the general plan.

OF 35 — Of course, I've seen my house [a dream house] . . . I've even walked past it . . . you go to the architect with an idea . . . of course, you've seen things you like in magazines . . . there are so many factors involved . . . obviously, if the architect shows me models, I'll think about them . . . but ultimately, *in principle*, you form an idea and you want that idea to be carried out . . .

I even recorded the following slip, which I considered to be highly significant.

OF 35 — *When you take your plans to the architect . . .*

Taken literally, this would mean that the plans were already fully worked out when the client went to the architect. In point of fact, of course, they would have to be translated into design drawings by the architect.

a — But what is an *architect*?

OF 35 — Well . . . he's someone who designs things . . . isn't he?

a — . . .

— An architect doesn't design things? . . . he does . . . he does design things? . . . he knows how to design, doesn't he? . . .

The plans have been decided upon, all that remains is for design drawings to be made from them, which will be done by the architect, who 'knows how to design', working from the plans brought to him by his client.

> — But when you take your plans to the architect *you do tend to listen to his advice* ...

OF 33 — Of course, for someone who knows about such matters ...

a — For someone who knows about such matters? ...

> — Yes, well ... an architect ... well, of course, we could have had it done by an architect, and it would doubtless have been done better ... **but not the plans** ... not the plans, because it was my husband who conceived the plans, and made a good job of them, but when it comes to the actual *construction*, he's far from being an expert ... he did it himself for financial reasons ...

a — An architect possesses technical knowledge?

> — Oh yes, I should say so, certainly ...

a — But as far as the plan was concerned? ...

> — As far as the plan was concerned, my husband was able to work that out without help from anyone ... anyway, the plans have been approved ... now ... I suppose it's not everyone who could do that ...

In one instance we even found that the interviewee knew nothing at all about the *architect*:

a — Le Corbusier built your house, didn't he?

M 8 — Yes, he did, he had it built by the architect. But it was his idea, of course. Poor man, if he'd had to do it all on his own ... but it was his idea ...

Le Corbusier: his style and 'style'

In Pessac the architect was Le Corbusier. I have already drawn attention to the effect that his personality may well have exerted on my study. But it also enabled me to establish the kind of views held by the occupants on architects in general and on such concepts as 'style' and 'modern architecture' which, incidentally, they discussed quite freely and without any prompting.

> **M 7** — *You have to realize* that his ideas are now being applied everywhere . . . low ceilings, terraces, small kitchens. Frankly, by now I quite like his conception, you know . . . and *besides* it's sturdy [the interviewee seemed to find a certain compensation in the strength of Le Corbusier's structures] . . . I notice that there are some new blocks which have just been built over there on the Arcachon road, and they're in the same style . . . he wanted to rebuild Agadir . . . in his own style, of course . . . a little personal perhaps for those times, but now I see that it's being taken up again . . . on the Arcachon road there is a settlement which was built five years back and it's in the same style as Pessac, exactly the same style, and really . . . this style is as good as most . . .

What really matters in a building or a cluster of buildings is not so much the quality of the style as the fact that there is a style:

> **a** — There is a style then?

> **OF 35** — Yes, of course there is, but it's not so easy to describe because . . . *we're not experts,* and then . . . but of course there is a style. In the first place this style arises out of the contrast with the neighbouring houses.

> **a** — What is its principal feature?

> — The walls . . . there's something rigid about it, something austere . . . *it's a cubist style.* It's not at all easy to form an assessment of this settlement because it is so dilapidated and the *dilapidation, coming on top of everything else,* is really too much . . . but an austere house like that, that might not be at all unpleasant . . . but I think I'd prefer a detached house . . .

M 7 — *Obviously, the style is not something that you are constantly aware of . . .*: if you go to some magnificent spot a number of times you get used to it . . . . etc.

The relationship between the architect, his style, the aesthetic quality of his building and the spontaneous reaction of the viewer is nicely defined in this last passage.

    s — What is this style?

    — Well . . . flat roofs, terraces, square houses in a 'Spanish' style [*a variation on the North African theme*] . . . If I had to start all over again I would do exactly the same things . . . Mark you, I don't think we have the right to change anything, but . . . because if I change the style of the roof, I change the style of the whole house . . . the design being what it is, essentially square, if you put a roof on top, you destroy the whole character of the house.

    s — You must preserve its character . . .

    — We must respect its character because the person who thought of doing it that way . . . was surely bound to be right . . . *there are styles more ridiculous than this one*: here people would call it an Arab style . . . but if you had to describe a high rise building you would probably say that it looked like a barracks . . .

In point of fact, this analogy with high rise buildings was not really relevant, for the new style was judged by comparison with traditional styles.

    F 15 — This cube may be very good but there are a number of functional mistakes . . . there's no protection for the building . . . the building is a cube and it is exposed to the wind in all directions . . .

    s — It is austere . . .

    — Yes, it is . . . there is nothing soft about the construction of the house . . . it is a perfect cube . . . with all that that implies in the way of rigidity, angularity and ugliness . . . it's very tidy, very neat and tidy, very well designed, but

. . . and, you know, *from an architectural point of view there is also an enormous drawback* because a cube . . . for example, when it rains this [*the window*] is just a sheet of water and there is no protection, there is not even an awning around the windows, they didn't even think of fitting a small concrete sill, which would have been very useful because the water would have been thrown away from the wall whilst, as it is, it is wearing it away, eroding it all the time, and that is how the buildings are being ruined: by the rain . . . it [the house] is exposed to every wind . . . it stands there like that . . . *square* to the wind!

It would seem that this particular occupant had fully grasped Le Corbusier's architectural conception but was by no means convinced of its functional value.

M 8 — Now that he is dead, you know, they are discovering that he was not so stupid after all . . . much the same as with Jules Verne . . . it's always been like that . . . people who are ahead of their times . . . if you suddenly think of a way of building houses that has never been tried before, people will say you're mad, and they'll keep on saying it . . . but **afterwards,** when you're dead, they'll discover that, when all is said and done . . . but if you're not dead, huh! . . . it's hardly worth your while to exhibit your work . . .

a — You think architecture is like painting in this respect? . . .

— Yes it is, you have to find a style . . . from the moment a young man finds a style . . . for his houses, and it doesn't really matter whether it's practical . . . but they must be based on something specific . . .

a — And architecture is like painting in this respect . . .

— Well no, architecture is different . . . it's defined . . . it already has a firm basis . . . in painting, if someone wants to produce a modern work, he can paint a ship that is completely unrecognizable . . . whereas if you wanted to build an abstract house . . . and you put a door in the roof . . . I don't quite know how to say this . . . you must be able to get into the house through a door, and if you put it in the roof . . .

a — Just the same, when this house was built, the public
tended to react in that way . . .

— Yes, of course, they wondered if he was mad . . .

a — Do you understand their reaction? . . .

— Yes, I understand it because I find that this young man
was very much ahead of his time . . .

a — People had the impression that he was putting lots of
doors in lots of roofs. They tended to think of him as a
second Picasso . . .

— Oh yes, indeed they did . . . it was his genre; they said:
'that man is completely mad, . . . placing a chimney in
the middle of the dining-room . . .', 'Well, what can you
expect, he's trying to make a name for himself' . . . but
I find . . . it was pretty intelligent of Le Corbusier to have
done that . . .

a — And what is 'style'? . . .

— Well now . . . something that . . . that no one has ever
been able to define . . . before Le Corbusier . . . it was a
genre . . . in his case, I'd say, it was individual . . .
Le Corbusier had an individual genre for building
houses . . .

a — What do you mean? Give me an example . . .

— First . . . he built cubes . . . I don't quite know how to say
this . . . . look, if you try to invent something,
you will never discover anything because in the final
analysis . . . you are merely repeating things that have
already been done . . . but you have to discover something new . . . and the moment you do so, then that's it,
your reputation is made . . . it's a little like modern music,
the 'jerk' and all that sort of thing; of course. You'll say
'that's like nothing on earth . . .' Fair enough . . . but by
comparison with the people . . . with the old people living
today, I find that normal; and you know what people said
when they first played the polka: 'they've gone too far',
'the younger generation is mad . . .', it amounts to the

same thing . . . mark you . . . things are moving a bit too fast nowadays . . .

a — What, for example ? . . .

— The times . . . everything ! . . . they are discovering too much all at once nowadays.

The interviewee then went on to discuss 'modern design':

— Look, these vases . . . they're modern.

a — But why are they modern ?

— Because they have no form . . . Look! How shall I put it ? . . . these candlesticks have no form, they only look as if they have . . . pieces of metal that have been beaten or hammered and chiselled, you see, and then . . . there's a bit of decorative work as well . . . someone just tried his hand . . . this was the result and it was used . . . to make a pair of candlesticks . . .

a — But it's not cubist, is it ? . . .

— It's . . . modern . . . the moment that . . . the sideboard over there is classical, it's not very old because old sideboards are always carved . . . but its classical none the less because it's unpretentious. The vase up there is also classical: if I want to depict a vase I draw a cone with a base ! . . . whereas that vase over there is full of twists and turns, there, you see, spirals everywhere, and so it's modern . . .

Clearly, modern design means different things to different generations. As we have just seen, young people tend to regard it as a kind of formal Baroque. But for the older generation modern design is much purer and much closer to the conceptions evolved by Le Corbusier, especially his conception of the machine.

M 19 — For my part, the one thing that pleases me about most modern buildings, the one thing, is the fact that they are so new and clean and orderly . . . to my mind that is the great advantage of modern design . . . but when modern buildings are allowed to grow old and dilapidated . . .

I find that absolutely abominable, fearful . . . because by
then everything that was attractive about the buildings
is destroyed, all that remains is a repellent reminder of
their original purity . . . the other kinds of houses, old
houses built of stone and so on . . . they can afford to
grow old, it just doesn't matter . . . but modern buildings
can't afford to grow old and, when they do, they have to
be kept in an impeccable state of repair . . . I expect
modern design to be clean, orderly and impeccable . . .
if it is not impeccable, it is worthless . . .

The temporal image of Pessac

This idea of 'modern buildings growing old' is extremely apposite.
It explains the position occupied by the Pessac settlement in time, for it
defines the temporal factor, which is one of the elements that go to make
up the urban image of the Q.M.F. But it would seem from the testimony
of the occupants that Le Corbusier's architecture has not stood the test
of time:

F 15 — I prefer old things, but I am not against modernism . . .
[*incidentally, later in the interview this occupant succeeded
in reconciling the 'old' and the 'new' when she described a
project for 'converting an old cupboard into a broom
cupboard'*] some modern things have been done very
well . . . of course, we have to distinguish between this
old modernism and present day modernism, which we
prefer, perhaps because it is new, but also because
research has been carried out . . . people have learnt from
experience . . . mistakes have been made and remedies
have been suggested . . . People have said: 'right! we did
that . . . very well! . . . but in the final analysis it wasn't
all that marvellous' . . . or 'it was troublesome' or 'it was
a useless impediment', 'so we'll change it, we'll try
something else instead . . .'

Clearly, as far as Pessac is concerned, Le Corbusier's architecture is an
example of 'old modernism'. As such, it could not lay claim to the durability vouchsafed by traditional architecture, nor could it draw on the
experience amassed by 'present day modernism'. 'Space', Gaston
Bachelard has observed, 'is like condensed time, its purpose is to con-
dense time'. Considered in this light, the urban space of Pessac serves no
purpose at all, for the architecture there contains no temporal element.

But there is a compensatory factor, one which was mentioned time and again in the interviews. This factor was the enormous strength of the Pessac houses, which enabled them to take root, so to speak, in both time and space. Lacking temporal security, the interviewees sought compensation in material security:

F 15 — The buildings here are very strong, much stronger than some of the ultramodern buildings, which seem to be very flimsy indeed! . . . Here you have an impression of solidity . . . in the first place, the houses are cubes . . . which gives an impression of solidity . . .

M 3 — We like the houses very much . . . at first they were subjected to severe criticism, but that was because people didn't know anything about them. You know, bombs were dropped here [*during the war*] and they withstood the blast . . . not like the houses over there . . . we had five bombs in the neighbourhood . . . they must be pretty strong . . .

a — What do you think of this house?

M 1 — I think . . . how shall I put it . . . that it's a . . . solid house . . . you don't see any cracks in the walls as you do in those new houses . . .

M 2 — And from a structural point of view here . . . *it's pretty good*, you know . . . it's strong . . . You want to know how strong these houses are: that house over there was blasted by a bomb; the terrace fell to the ground but wasn't demolished and the staircase remained standing. I tell you . . . huh! you want to know if it's strong . . . I'll say it's strong . . . and, you know, I wanted to cut into the walls . . . well, I tell you . . . I came across iron bars . . . lots of them . . . and when they tell you it's reinforced concrete, well . . . take it from me, it's reinforced all right . . . before that falls down, huh, when all the other houses have fallen down, mine will still be standing, that's for sure!

'It's amazing, the things
they've done . . .'
Le Corbusier

8
The interviews:
comparison with Le Corbusier's
architectural conception

Standardization

According to Le Corbusier's own testimony, standardization was the
most important single aspect of the Pessac project. But, surprisingly,
the question of uniformity was scarcely mentioned in the course of the
interviews. Doctor M . . ., who had been a municipal councillor during
the construction period, and M. Vrinat, the director of works, had told
me that the uniform appearance of the houses had not been badly received and had not contributed to the unfavourable reaction of the
original occupants. I found this information interesting enough in view
of the polemics which have been – and still are – conducted in architectural circles on the conflict between standardization and individuality.
Later I shall be considering the process of 'individuation' which has
made it possible to achieve a remarkable synthesis of these two opposing
factors.

In the course of the interviews only one person, a young man 18 years
of age, developed this subject at any length. But his interest is accounted
for by the fact that his next door neighbour was regarded as the local
expert on Le Corbusier. This neighbour was the one man in Pessac who
knew and was able to explain how and why Le Corbusier had done what
he had done.[1]

---

[1] M.B., an animal sculptor, had accompanied Le Corbusier during one of his last
visits to the Q.M.F. and consequently was considered to be a 'connoisseur'. I was
told by one of the occupants: 'Go and see M.B. . . ., he will be able to give you
explanations that we could never give you. He knows about these things; he's a

Thus we find Le Corbusier describing his conception to M.B., who explained it to the young man's parents, who in turn explained it to him. But, although this interviewee's opinions were based on a mixture of personal observations and hearsay evidence, they are no less interesting for that:

> **M 8** — The rooms in these houses are all the same, yet not one of them has the same layout as its neighbour . . . But I don't understand why. None is the same . . . Of course, it's better like that . . . like that, with none of them being the same, they stand out more . . . Because no two houses are the same, you notice every single house . . . whereas, if they were all the same, you wouldn't notice them at all. This place . . . it's a proper settlement . . . even though no two houses are the same: every house has its garden, but no two houses are aligned in the same way . . . I repeat that he has built no two houses exactly the same . . . That's one of his ideas [*This statement shows the kind of influence exerted by M.B.*]. But it's still a settlement because the houses are similar . . . although not the same: it is a settlement because the houses all resemble one another and were built by the same man. I suppose that is what you would call a settlement.

> **s** — That means that you have detached houses, individual houses and a settlement all in one.

> — Yes, you have, haven't you. And that's what I like about it here. I don't think it can be very pleasant to live in the same sort of house as your neighbour. Look, *that house over there is not the same as this one, which makes us feel superior, you see.* And our neighbour feels that his house is superior to ours, and so on. This way everyone thinks that his house is better than anyone else's . . . For example, we get more light in the morning than our neighbour, but he has more later on, which balances things up . . . I don't know how to explain it to you . . . but the point is that, although the houses are the same, the layout of the rooms is different. For example, take the house where a friend

bit in that line himself.' It was due to the influence of this neighbour that the young man's parents had a partition removed, which had been erected by the previous occupants. Their neighbour explained to them, as he later explained to me, that by erecting a partition their predecessors had cut off the view of the staircase, thus destroying Le Corbusier's design.

of mine lives: in his house this room, which is our dining-room, is their kitchen . . . and they don't have a dining room; instead they have an area that can serve either as a room or as a hall like the one we have here. [Basically] the rooms have been switched round. And then upstairs one of the rooms . . . instead of being a bedroom as it is here . . . is an office . . . It's like that in all the houses . . . I don't know why he arranged things like that . . .; no doubt he was anticipating something, although I don't know what . . . we'll see . . . perhaps the future course of events . . . He must have had something in mind . . .

— For my part, *I don't like houses that look alike* . . . but, although these look alike, they are not the same . . . that's the good thing . . . that's the good thing about them: these houses here [*the aligned houses*] are all more or less the same, which I don't like . . . Here, on the other hand, no two houses are aligned in the same way, so they aren't the same; and that I do like. Each house is like all the others, and yet it is not the same . . . The others are all the same: their terraces are all laid out in the same direction, whereas here, you see, one terrace points in one direction whilst the next points in the opposite direction. . .

It is strange that the personal implications of standardization should not have been broached in any of the other interviews. As it was, this young man was the only person to mention the personal touches which he had given his house – such as the Venetian blinds and the decorative facing (see illustration 58) – and which he regarded as an absolute necessity, or to discuss the scope offered by Le Corbusier's design for personal expression on the part of the occupants. The other interviewees made no reference whatsoever to this question. Le Corbusier, however, was well aware of the need to cater for the individuality of the Pessac residents, as has already been pointed out in the section on 'isolation'. Hence his attempt to provide different interior designs (which he aptly referred to as a 'game of lotto').

F 3 — This system of having one house facing the front and the other facing the back, I find that very good because you never have trouble with your neighbours; when I'm in my kitchen at the back my neighbour is in her kitchen at the front . . . I go out at the back to my dustbins and

so on, and she – she goes out the front . . . you know, we
often spend a whole day at home without seeing one
another . . . Although we're all packed together like this,
you still have the feeling that you're on your own . . .

F 10 — When I am in my dining-room, if I have guests, the sound
of our voices will carry towards the garden . . . if the
lady next door has guests, their voices will carry towards
the road . . .

Of course, the fact that the vast majority of those interviewed failed to
mention the uniformity of the houses does not mean that they were not
influenced by it. On the other hand, we have already seen that the
apparently obvious explanation for the modifications carried out by the
occupants, namely that they were trying to lend a personal note to what
they considered to be impersonal architecture, is too simplistic. Even
if it is not entirely false, it certainly needs to be subjected to a more
searching analysis. This I shall be doing later.

*The 'machine to live in', functionalism, rationalism, the discrepancy
between thought and action in the architect and the occupants*

We must now turn back for a moment to the two sequences of interviews on 'modern design' and 'modernism'. In the case of 'modernism' –
the word is inappropriate but it was the one used in the interview – we
were told that this entailed, above all else, the elimination of anything
'troublesome', 'impeding' or 'useless'. In other passages of the same
interview the Q.M.F. were criticized because they were 'not logical', 'not
rational' and 'not functional'. It would seem, therefore, that the
functionalism and rationalism extolled by Le Corbusier but found to be
sadly neglected in Pessac are the principal qualities which people expect
to find in modern architecture. Traditional architecture, on the other
hand, is expected to possess quite different qualities. And it seemed to
me that the necessary synthesis between the old and the new was created by this same interviewee when she described her project for 'converting an old cupboard into a broom cupboard' . . . The lack of cupboard space in Pessac posed a real problem for this housewife and pin-
pointed the need for functionalism in modern design. Le Corbusier's
rationalist evangelization of architecture appears to have achieved its
purpose. But his architecture does not! In the article by Le Corbusier
from which I have already quoted, the following sentence appears
immediately after a series of quotations from his earlier writings: 'What
this conception shows us is that we must first try to eliminate all *useless*

110

and troublesome features, which impede freedom of movement, compli-
cate maintenance work and tie up capital to no good purpose . . .' The
words in italics are exactly the same as those used by the Pessac housewife to describe the deficiencies of Le Corbusier's houses . . .

Of course, these expressions were applied to functional and therefore
mainly internal features. However, a second interviewee insisted that
modern design must be 'clean, orderly and impeccable', which are, of
course, primarily external characteristics. Interestingly enough, this conception – which was formulated with the Q.M.F. in mind – also describes
the principal aesthetic properties of the machine as defined by Le
Corbusier: '. . . A type of beauty based on the purity of its forms and the
precision of its performance. Machines replace work done by hand;
their operations are smooth, regular and perfect; cylinders have the
absolute quality of a theory.' But in Pessac, as on many other of Le
Corbusier's building sites, the construction work was far from perfect:
'The walls are out of square . . .'

The cleanliness, orderliness and impeccability insisted on by this
interviewee (**M 19,** p.103) must also be considered in the light of his
earlier reactions to the different materials used in modern architecture.

> **M 19** — Amongst modern materials I like glass, metal, steel,
> aluminium; I don't like concrete.

When Le Corbusier refers to the 'smoothness' of machines this surely
conjures up an image of burnished steel. And yet, not only the houses
in Pessac, but virtually all of Le Corbusier's buildings are made of
concrete, unfinished concrete for the most part, in which the marks of
the shuttering are still clearly visible and which acquires its animation
from the coarseness and imperfections of its texture. The discrepancy
that we find here between the architect's statements – which reflect his
original intention – and his actions is by no means rare in Le Corbusier's case. Meanwhile, the Pessac resident found that his requirements,
which were based on the same values as those extolled by Le Corbusier,
were not satisfied by the architect of the Q.M.F. Here the architect's intention was belied by his acts. But then, we have already noted the
ambiguity of Le Corbusier's 'machine' in an earlier chapter.

By a curious coincidence we find a similar discrepancy between
thought and action in the case of the resident. An intellectual with apparently little regard for material things, he seems quite content with an
old cheap car and an untidy house, in which electric light cables are
strung across the passageway and the walls 'could do with a lick of
distemper'. Strange surroundings for a man concerned with the need
for cleanliness and orderliness! Clearly, this occupant applied separate
standards, which are hinted at by certain phrases which he used. The

following phrase, for example, occurred frequently in the course of the interview:

> **M 19** — There are *two levels* . . . the first level . . .
>
> — . . . there again, there are *two levels* . . .

A second interviewee, again an intellectual, also applied separate standards:

> **M 22** — What does my wife think? . . . well now . . . well, *since my wife is a lecturer* I'll answer your question under two separate headings: *as an intellectual* I suppose you'd say, although the term is pedantic . . . she rates the house highly . . . not as highly as I do . . . but highly enough . . . of course, *I'm speaking on an intellectual level* . . .
>
> **a** — And on the other level . . .
>
> — Well, *on the other level*, I must admit that for the first two years she was not exactly enamoured of Le Corbusier . . . for reasons which were not directly connected with . . . well, primarily on account of the heating and the badly fitting windows . . . *the point of view of the mother* . . . of the housewife . . .

We see, therefore, that people live in houses on two different levels. To be more precise: a house is firstly something that we think about, something to which we adopt an aesthetic attitude, and secondly something that we live in. This duality was also clearly expressed in the prospectus which was discussed in Chapter 1 and which was, of course, addressed to *non-residents*.

> 'All you have to do is ask the people who live in our villas how they feel about them and what it feels like to be living in them.'

What a person feels about a house and what it feels like to be living in a house are two different things, the second of which, at least, can only be assessed by the occupant.

In a manner of speaking, therefore, a house leads a dual existence: on the one hand it is an object of intellectual and aesthetic analysis whilst on the other hand it is a container in which people live their lives.

In the first case it is the exterior that is usually the major consideration, in the second it is the interior.

As far as the occupants are concerned, of course, the architect is not necessarily responsible for both of these aspects. Basically, they expect him to design a container, whose internal layout they have already determined.

The alterations: the 'construction game'

We have already seen that there was a discrepancy between the intentions and actions of the architect on the one hand and the statements and behaviour of the occupants on the other. This discrepancy, which we have encountered on various occasions in the course of this study, is of an order similar to the distinction made by the occupants when they formed alternative assessments of their houses:

> — '. . . at first . . . and then afterwards . . .'

> — '. . . from the outside . . . on the inside . . .'

> — '. . . when you first arrive . . . when you live there . . .'

> — '. . . how they feel about them . . . what it feels like to be living in them . . .'

> — '. . . at an intellectual level . . . at a practical level . . .'

We now have to consider the alterations carried out by the occupants, which were of course the original point of departure for this whole study. But how does one approach this problem? After all, these alterations reflect the occupants' behaviour which, as we have just seen, was often at variance with their statements. Moreover, as we saw in Chapter 6, it was often extremely difficult to establish the precise reasons which had prompted particular alterations.

In the end I came to the conclusion that the only viable solution was to adopt a much more general approach and so, instead of trying to analyse individual alterations in detail, I decided to consider them as an *ensemble*. This was, in fact, the very approach I had adopted when investigating the local lean-to houses, whose real importance lay not in any particular alterations effected by their occupants but in the tendency revealed by the people of the Bordeaux region to extend their houses by means of back additions, a tendency that is so pronounced that these back additions have virtually become a standard feature.

Thus, instead of trying to prepare a complete list of the alterations that had been made in the Q.M.F., which would have shown how many houses had been equipped with corridors and so on, I contented myself with producing a number of schemas, all of which represented actual situations but which were intended to demonstrate, not the precise nature of the alterations that had been effected, but their variety.

Certainly, it is of interest to know that, where a corridor has been introduced, there is a strong possibility that the occupant was influenced by recollections of the lean-to house. But how much more important to know that, like the traditional lean-to house, Le Corbusier's villas were *capable of being altered and were in fact altered.* Within the context of the Bordeaux region, where it has long been established practice to extend dwelling houses by means of back additions and to litter the countryside with outbuildings, it is surely far more interesting to observe a general tendency on the part of the Pessac residents to order their own houses than to furnish fragmentary analyses of their conversions based on functional and other criteria. At this point the phenomenon of Pessac acquires a new meaning, which also makes our enquiry more meaningful; because once we begin to consider the situation in general terms we find that, far from revealing discrepancies, the interviews and our own observations combine to produce a clear picture of the many opportunities provided by Le Corbusier's architectural conception for subsequent conversions and alterations. Indeed, one of the essential features of this conception is the fact that it *facilitated* and, to a certain extent, even *encouraged* such alterations.

One's immediate impression of Le Corbusier's Pessac project in its present state is that it must have been an architectural failure, since otherwise it would never have been transformed to such an extent. In point of fact, however, we see from a more careful analysis of this phenomenon that, far from constituting a failure, the alterations are an entirely positive feature.

This is clearly borne out both by the testimony of the occupants and by my own observations:

> **M 20** — I bought this house in five minutes flat: I didn't like the outside at all, but I saw its potential at once . . . It's the sort of house where you could introduce all manner of combinations.

> **F 10** — If I owned this house, I know I'd make a number of alterations and I'd certainly build a corridor . . . I know I'd run the corridor along the whole length of

the house and I'd extend this room, the way people do nowadays, by building a large bay window overlooking the garden . . . There are lots of alterations to be made in these houses . . . To my mind, there are as many different styles of architecture as there are houses . . . It could be . . .

s — Do you think it is one of the characteristics of these houses that they can be . . .

— converted? [*Note the non-directive approach, which lends greater significance to the reply.*] I don't know whether it occurred to Le Corbusier twenty-five years ago, but it's quite an easy matter to convert them, in fact you can do more or less as you please . . . I have no idea what . . . whether it occurred to him, but you can certainly rearrange things to suit yourself . . . You can make two rooms out of this one by dividing it down the middle . . . which would be completely in line with present day design . . . Oh! there are all sorts of possible arrangements . . . You know, my husband has made thirty-six different designs.

a — Has he other plans?

— Oh yes. For our part, we've already made four different plans [*by using the phrase 'For our part' the interviewee clearly indicates that others are also preoccupied with such plans.*] . . . we've not really made up our minds about this room . . . but we know what we'd do about the others; the small rear room, for example, could be eliminated, then you could extend the kitchen and that would give you a corridor extending right up to the living room . . . and you'd also have a large kitchen . . . it's one possibility . . . you could use the entrance for a garage . . . and if you didn't want a garage you could build a washhouse . . . you could even turn it into a bathroom and W.C. . . . and upstairs, well there you could enlarge the bedroom by breaking into the small bathroom and you could use what's left of the bathroom for a dressing room, which would give you a pretty big bedroom. Incidentally, that's what my parents have done . . . [*the parents also live in the district*].

The convertibility of the houses was sometimes clearly appreciated:

M 22 — But there is a certain . . . flexibility which makes it possible to adapt to new needs . . . to introduce new elements into a framework that was not really designed to receive them. . .

And sometimes clearly expressed:

M 19 — But, you know, what I like about the house from an architectural point of view . . . from the point of view of amenities [*note the definition of architecture in terms of amenities*] . . . although I doubt if he designed it with that in mind because I have the feeling that he was pretty *rigid* in his outlook . . . and I can imagine that he'd be rather upset to see what people have done to these houses (justifiably so for the most part), but what I like . . . what I find interesting . . . is that the basic design makes it possible for the house to be *adapted* to its occupants instead of the occupants having to adapt to the house . . . for example . . . my entrance hall used to be a bare space . . . that [*the office*] was a garage . . . hm . . . upstairs, well! there used to be a living room which took up the whole floor . . . so, depending on their needs and wishes, the occupants of these houses can convert the garage into a room, they can erect a partition, over there, to make another room, they can block off the staircase . . . to make a room . . . hm . . . I found that extremely interesting: you create, as it were, a . . . significant volume where, originally, there hadn't even been a five-room flat, as it were . . . that enables the occupants . . . successive generations of occupants . . . to make their own changes . . . whereas in some houses . . . you take what you're given . . . and you have to live with it, you can't convert anything at all . . . [*here*] the houses are readily convertible . . . because, take the terrace, well . . . some people have made it into a room . . . [*and the interviewee launched into a description of other possible conversions*].

M 1 — On the other side it used to be open to the elements . . . I closed it up because . . . we're a large family and I tried to provide the best accommodation I could.

a — So, in point of fact, you can do what you like in these houses? . . .

— Yes. Look . . . a house that . . . this used to be the kitchen here and there were two more rooms plus the living room . . . but now I have three rooms, this kitchen area here . . . and the living room . . . which is the same size as before . . . so you see basically . . . it's a four-room flat . . .

The present residents of the Q.M.F. have evidently realized – better than the residents of similar settlements elsewhere – that it is preferable for a house to be adapted to its occupants than for the occupants to have to adapt to their house. This realization, which is an important one, seems to have been prompted by the sight of the many conversions that have been carried out in the district:

M 3 — As I told them . . . *do it for yourselves*, don't convert anything for your children because, no matter who moves in when you leave, whether it's your children or strangers, *they're bound to pull something down.* They won't like things the way they are. You've put the door there, they'll want it over there! You've closed up a wall to make . . . they'll build a door in it or else knock it down to make a larger room (and that's happened before now): there are houses down there, the people took out a large partition wall, made a large kitchen and thought it was absolutely marvellous . . . and now, huh . . . the good man has put the partition back, so that the kitchen's the same size as it was before, in order to make an extra room for one of his children . . . you see? . . . people will always make changes . . . there's nothing 'amazing' about it. No . . . *any house, no matter how well designed it may be, will never completely suit the family that goes to live in it* . . . There's always something that needs to be changed. It does no harm . . . and it's good for trade . . . I've lived here for twenty years now and I've seen it happen time and again; there are houses which have had three or four different owners, and they've all pulled down something or other and then rebuilt, each according to his taste . . . it's a way of life . . .

But the conversions, or rather the idea for the conversions, also seem to have been prompted in part by the size of the rooms, which appears to have taken many of the occupants by surprise. The following extract is from an interview with a woman who had moved into her house only three months before; it shows how the dimensions of the various rooms led quite naturally to ideas for their conversion:

F 15 — You know, lots of people say: 'How big it is!' When they first enter the house it strikes them as big . . . But, when they go into the dressing room, they say: 'Oh, but this dressing room is minute!' Whenever there are two of us in there, we get in one another's way, which shows how small it is . . . The large room . . . is very large . . . Incidentally, they call it **the** large room, but the real point about it is that it is **large.** You can see for yourself . . . it is large . . . that's a large area, isn't it! . . . the small room is . . . a bit too small . . . a little bit! a bit too small! you'd need to . . . although . . . I rather like large rooms . . . But . . . if you wanted to rationalize it, you'd need to take away a quarter of the space from here and add it on over there, and then you'd have two well-balanced rooms . . . That would make a living room . . . at a pinch, the kitchen could be left as it is . . . or else this could be left, in which case the verandah would have to go – it serves no useful purpose anyway – and . . . as for the W.C.s, which I find quite unnerving, it would be . . . For example, you could have . . . this would be partitioned off on one side with a large entrance door in the partition wall, then partitioned off in the middle to make a second room, because otherwise the room would be too large to serve any useful purpose, which would give you two rooms in all . . . One of these would communicate with the kitchen, the other – for which you could soon find a use – with this room here . . . So there you are! Once that had been done then, I think, the interior would more or less match the exterior . . .

We must now consider a number of statements made by the occupants of houses in a settlement about three or four kilometres from Pessac, which also have a bearing on this study. Although they were not built until 1960, these houses are very similar to those designed by Le Corbusier for the Q.M.F. They are, in fact, the houses referred to on p.99 by the Pessac resident (**M 7**), who pointed out that people are still building in the style evolved by Le Corbusier.

Amongst other things, we asked these householders whether they had thought of making any alterations to their homes. From the replies to this question – which was put directly since, otherwise, the subject would never have been mentioned – we learnt that, although many would have liked to do so, nobody had seriously considered the possibility:

> **a** — Have you any plans for rearranging your house?

> **OF 29** — I don't think it would be possible to rearrange very much in this house . . . On the outside, perhaps . . . If I had had an end house . . . I might have tried to do something about the garage. Turn it into an extra room; some people have done that.

In another house we asked a young person:

> **a** — Have your parents done anything to the house?

> **OC 34** — Oh, they've repapered the rooms, but that's all . . .

> **a** — Have you built on at the back of the house?

> — Yes, a wine cellar . . . We use it as a lumber room, you know. Nearly all our neighbours have done the same . . .

We asked another occupant:

> **a** — Do you intend to carry out any conversions?

> **OM 30** — Yes, but . . . not immediately . . . I think . . . because, you see, if I build a corridor, it will take up half the room . . . I think, when all is said and done . . . I'll leave things as they are . . . you can't do much here in the way of conversions; it's all been worked out very carefully . . . they've obviously cut down on space all the way round in order to economize, you know . . .

These houses certainly lacked the spaciousness that is one of the characteristics of the Pessac villas:

F 6 — There's space . . . plenty of space. That's why people have knocked down partition walls, realigned them and generally rearranged things . . .

But, quite apart from its quantitative significance, there is also a qualitative aspect to space, which allowed the Pessac residents considerable latitude in the arrangement of their homes:

a — What would you do?

M 13 — I would rearrange the house in such a way that it was quite modern . . . *either modern or traditional* . . . you can do either in these houses . . .

a — You can do either in these houses? . . .

— Yes, either . . .

a — But how is that possible? . . .

— Because of the layout . . . because . . . because of the way they're built. Take the terrace, I'd lay out a summer garden . . . over there, under the stairs, I'd have a bar . . . over the way the 'X's' have *a superb house* . . . *they've converted it into three flats. Of course, he's a professional* . . .

Pessac: an example of open construction

If we compare the various interiors evolved by the occupants with Le Corbusier's original design it is immediately apparent that his conception readily lent itself to subsequent modification. The diagrams reproduced opposite show the different conversions that we discovered in one of the three types of houses in Pessac. Clearly, the range of possible and actual combinations is very wide. But then, according to one of the occupants, the architect's task is to provide an infrastructure, a basic framework, within which the occupants would be able to give a more or less free rein to their own ideas in both a qualitative (combinatory) and quantitative (spatial) sense.

From a quantitative point of view the *total* amount of useful space provided in each house was in line with contemporary practice. We have already seen that it was approximately the same as the amount

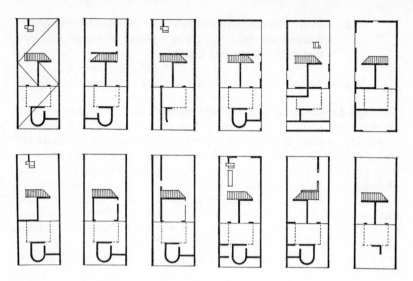

Le Corbusier's original design is on the top left.

provided by Oud in Weissenhof. But where Le Corbusier departed from normal practice was in his insistence on extremely small areas for purely functional rooms such as kitchens and bathrooms. In these rooms, which he regarded as 'laboratories' and which were inspired by the galleys and bathrooms in ocean liners and Pullman cars, every object had its proper place and not a square centimetre was wasted. The space saved in this way was then used to enlarge the other rooms in the house. Thus, the dining room – which incorporated the staircase – measured 25 square metres. This type of layout was well described by one of the occupants (**F 15,** p.118): 'dressing room – minute', 'large room – large', 'small room – a bit too small'.

Incidentally, although many of the occupants complained that the terrace was wasted space (because it was not a proper room), in point of fact it was space that Le Corbusier had saved, for his ingenious layout had enabled him to exploit the natural division between the houses and use it for this purpose. The other complaint frequently heard in Pessac, namely that the large rooms were too large, seems to stem from the fact that people have now grown accustomed to the lack of space that is one of the principal characteristics of present-day dwellings:

F 10 — You can make two rooms out of this one by dividing it down the middle . . . which would be completely in line with present-day design . . .

M 1 — basically . . . it's a four-room flat . . .

Although Le Corbusier undoubtedly played a part, primarily through his writings, in the development of the small-scale modern dwelling (which is based on the principles underlying steamship and Pullman car accommodation), he did not apply this formula unilaterally and – in Pessac at least – it would be quite wrong to say that the amount of space provided was limited. In later projects, it is true, this was less obviously the case. But in the Q.M.F., although some of the rooms were much smaller than elsewhere, others were very much larger. From an aesthetic point of view this produced an interesting contrast between the different volumes, which I found impressive but which was scarcely mentioned in the interviews. The quality of the rooms is partly determined by their size.

But the spatial quality of the houses was not *rigidly* determined, which is what we would expect in so far as Le Corbusier's villas were not conceived as purely functional containers. This emerged quite clearly in Chapter 3, where the Pessac project was compared with Oud's Weissenhof scheme, which was seen to be much more functional in every way. Thus, the strictly functional use of space that one would have expected from a 'machine to live in' is far less apparent in Pessac than elsewhere; and although it was due in no small measure to Le Corbusier's influence that functionalism has become one of the general characteristics of present-day dwellings, it was as a writer and not as an architect that he made this influence felt.

The lack of spatial definition in Pessac is clearly demonstrated by the sort of terms used to describe different living areas. For example, Le Corbusier called one particular room a parlour (*parloir*), a word which is so vague that it can mean virtually anything. And, in fact, we find that it really is extremely difficult to put a name to this particular room, which fulfils different functions for different occupants since every second terraced house in Pessac, it will be remembered, faces in the opposite direction. Occasionally, the occupants also used expressions which were every bit as vague as Le Corbusier's and which consequently also helped to demonstrate the lack of spatial definition:

'Here . . . we had the rest-room . . .'

The room referred to by this occupant was used by others as an entrance hall, an office, a bedroom, a living room and, in one case, as a hairdressing salon, which was later converted into a 'studio' when the hairdresser retired from business.

> **M 1** — We blocked it off ourselves . . . the little studio can
> always be used as a room, if necessary . . . it's not
> really a room, of course, it just . . . makes an extra
> room . . . in an emergency . . .

The same sort of thing happened with the garages, which were converted into rooms, kitchens, workshops for artisans and handymen, offices, wine stores and so on. This is hardly surprising for the houses in Pessac were built to accommodate workers in 1925, at which time very few workers owned motor-cars.

But it was not only Le Corbusier's spatial conception that was untrammelled. So too was his structural conception, which was based on the five 'key points' of modern architecture proclaimed by him at the time of the Pessac project: wide windows, roof gardens, stilts, open façades and open plan interiors.

The first four of these points involve areas that are naturally *open* in both a material and a figurative sense. Thus, the wide windows, which were made possible in the first instance by the fact that modern façades no longer have to be loadbearing (hence their designation as 'open façades'), could easily be reduced in size whereas it would have been much more difficult to enlarge narrow windows. By the same token, both the terrace and the area beneath the stilts lent themselves readily to conversion, for it is undoubtedly much easier to add a roof to a terrace than to remove a section of roof in order to make a terrace. Although the conversions of these naturally 'open' spaces were purely material features, they were none the less carried out in Pessac and must therefore be taken into account.

Le Corbusier's fifth 'key point' was his 'open plan' interior design.

Although this type of design undoubtedly allowed the occupants considerable latitude, which they did not hesitate to use, this will certainly not have been Le Corbusier's intention. His open plan design was undoubtedly prompted by the desire to create an architecturally satisfactory interior and not just a rough and ready setting which the occupants could adapt at will. Once again we come up against the discrepancy between Le Corbusier's intentions – as revealed in his writings – and his acts – as represented by his finished works.

Comparison with the group discussion

The impression created by Le Corbusier in his writings is essentially the same as the conception underlying the group discussion. Although the group was concerned primarily with the relative merits of 'open' or 'free' architecture on the one hand and 'closed' or 'finished' architecture on the other, everyone was agreed that Le Corbusier's architecture was essentially 'closed' or 'finished'. It would seem, therefore, that the popular impression of Le Corbusier's architecture – the impression given in his writings – is diametrically opposed to the impression created by his actual works and, more especially, by his Pessac project.[2] To convince ourselves of this we need only compare a few extracts from the group discussion with a few extracts from the interviews.

   B — I would like to point out that prior to our own epoch family houses, i.e. houses for private individuals, were not architect designed. It seems to me that this provides us with a means of approaching the role of the architect, who at present finds himself on the brink of a chaotic situation. *The role of the architect is not to finish a house* but simply to prepare it for the people who are going to live in it, using prefabricated components which will enable him to fit it out in such a way that these people will feel at home and will be prevented, as far as possible, from making any mistakes that would introduce a discordant note, when they come to arrange the different living areas, to build partitions and to design the general layout of the interior. [*There is a slight contradiction in the suggestion that the occupants should be prevented from making any mistakes.*]

   M — All architects are agreed on the need for flexibility of design; what they have to do is allow for such flexibility from the outset . . . if a design is able to satisfy the needs of A whilst a second design is able to satisfy the needs of both A and B, then the second design is the better, there can be no doubt about that.

   a — But do architects consider the question of how to satisfy the needs of A or B? . . .

   M — I'm sure they do . . .

   [2] This contradiction is also revealed by the interview reproduced on p.116 (**M 19**).

a — Did Le Corbusier, for example, consider that question?
... Apart from the fact that he wanted to pressurize
people, did he really offer them a choice between A
and B? ...

M — He may have pressurized them to some extent, he
certainly wanted to pressurize them because essentially
... what I mean to say is that at the time people
didn't want what Le Corbusier had to offer ... it
didn't meet the needs of a young couple moving into
one of his houses ... by no means ... It is, of course,
perfectly true that he failed to create the necessary
flexibility, such as we might have provided today,
perhaps because of the setbacks he had encountered;
but he was very sure of himself, that is a quality that
we have to recognize in him; he had a certain strength
which enabled him to accomplish his life's work; you may
object to his buildings, but they are there for all that,
and it was this strength that made him disregard the
need for flexibility ... He was sure that his solution
was right and it simply did not occur to him that there
could be an alternative ...

Let us now turn briefly to the prospectus:

Layout for the Interior:
'The interiors of the villas have not been completely
finished, partly in order to avoid any deterioration
whilst they are standing empty and partly in order to
benefit from the provisions of the law of 3 August
1926, which stipulates (in Article 18) that houses sold
in a partially finished condition are to be exempt from
the 7% conveyancing tax. However, the amount of
work that remains to be done is not significant and
purchasers will only have to wait for one or two weeks
before taking possession of their villas.'

So far the reasons advanced in the prospectus for the unfinished state
of the villas are functional and economic. But later we are told:

'As for the gardens and terraces, here we prefer to
allow the individual to use his own judgement and
imagination; but if they wish purchasers may consult the
plans evolved by M. Le Corbusier and M. Jeanneret.'

125

We see, therefore, that, for whatever reasons, the houses were unfinished when handed over to their original occupants:

> **M 8** — I like the 'X's' house, because they've done everything the way they wanted . . . I find that where a house is concerned they should do all the basic work . . . but it's a waste of time finishing it . . . and then, when the boy takes it over, he'll rearrange it in his own way, to suit himself . . . these houses are unfinished . . . at first it was dismal, everything was grey . . . now we've arranged things, it's all right . . .

> **a** — So the occupant finishes the house himself . . .

> — Yes, that's right. He has his house built and then he finishes it . . . that's the right way . . .

In Pessac the occupants were actually obliged to work on their houses themselves:

> **M 19** — In a house like this, you need to be a handyman, then there's no problem . . .

> **F 6** — *You have to* know how to arrange it . . . *you have to* know how to make the most of it, you see . . . otherwise the houses are very pleasant . . . *and strong.*

And so the basic assumptions made by the members of the group were contradicted by the experience of the occupants:

> **B** — I want to go back to a point I was making a moment ago. I firmly believe that people don't want to have their houses finished for them. But in Pessac *the houses were finished* and in this connexion I would like to point out once again that Le Corbusier was a pioneer . . . because the architectural forms which he evolved, which he created, were different, in general terms at least, from those which had existed before. There was a period of adaptation, after which the people began to realize – and so too did other people elsewhere – that, with their standardized volumes, the houses that had been provided for them . . . certainly had a restrictive effect and were *likely to pose difficulties.* *I imagine that the failure of the Pessac project was due*

to those difficulties, and our professional attitude is
lamentable because we are producing architecture in
which we impose our will on our clients; *we are in a
sense the fascists of the building industry* because we
build one cell, then add a second, a third, fourth, fifth,
because we impose *predetermined and perfected
volumes* reflecting an average sensitivity which,
however, never reflects the sensitivity of the people who
are going to live [in the houses] . . .

It would seem that little progress has been made in this respect since
1925 for this speaker then went on to ask the same question that Le
Corbusier had asked himself in Pessac.

B — With all the modern techniques that we have at our
disposal is it not possible to provide more diversified
dwelling places, using standardized, mass-produced
components of wood, aluminium, iron, bronze or
concrete? . . .

At this point I feel that it would be useful to reproduce a lengthy extract from the discussion, in which two of the participants commented
on the 'construction game':

E — Usually, when things get really bad, there is a safety
valve of one sort or another; the problems of living
constitute a sort of constant, and when people are no
longer able to tolerate a particular situation, they try
to find an outlet; the outlet discovered by town
dwellers is camping. Perhaps camping is too mobile,
perhaps it is unhygienic, but it does provide an
alternative to our sclerotic towns, which came into
existence when those Titans produced their solid,
cuboid, concrete creations, which are not only rigid in
themselves but are also subject to rigid regulations,
whereby the maximum amount of cupboard space
allowed is 4 square metres; and this applies even if
you have to accommodate twenty Breton wardrobes
. . . for ten years now I have been arguing that it is
perfectly feasible, from a technical point of view, to
employ the 'construction game' system without any
set plan, without any set rules, simply by using one's
common sense. And since people are not naturally
self-destructive, sooner or later they are going to take

practical steps to perfect their culture . . . they have already managed to dress themselves more or less decently, and the day will come when they will manage to live more or less decently as well, it's a question of education. And now that we are faced with the problem of leisure or, as I prefer to call it, the problem of idleness, this would be an excellent solution.

M — The 'construction game' system and all that it implies is fine. Nobody objects to it.

E — Then why isn't it being implemented? What you have on that piece of paper (*Pessac*) is not a 'construction game'. My children can do better than that with their *Lego*, which is far more complex. It is the so-called originality which pervades this bombastic nonsense that is so harmful because it has made people believe in something that doesn't exist.

a — Le Corbusier once made a very interesting observation when talking about Pessac: *one could build beautifully designed houses, always provided the tenant was prepared to change his outlook* . . . What are we to make of that? . . .

M — To my mind that means that the tenant is to be pressurized, that is the only possible meaning. I believe there is an American architect by the name of Wright, whose talent is undisputed but whose clients have never been satisfied with his work.

The discussion then reverted to the question of materials: it was suggested that, because of its weight, concrete precluded all possibility of a *mobile* solution.

E — It is time we were using 'construction games'. I've been proposing this for the past ten years . . .

M — It's all very well to propose it. But is your proposition practical? . . .

E — Of course it's practical . . . there are [self-appointed] guardians everywhere who insist that at least 50 kilogrammes of iron must be used for every 1000

128

kilogrammes of concrete whereas one could build a
house perfectly well, like Fuller for example, with 17
or even 15 kilogrammes.

M — We always work our way back to concrete, but that
isn't the real problem.

E — Let's not play with words . . . What is immobility,
what is rigidity? Is a large stone that weighs 500
kilogrammes mobile or immobile? It's all a question
of weight . . . I realize that this is bringing the
discussion down to a pretty low level; but what is
mobile? Anything I can pick up. For example, this
table is more or less mobile although not as mobile
as this object that I am holding in my hand . . .

We have already seen that the components of the Pessac houses were
not exactly light and mobile ('they're strong' . . .). Consequently, the
fact that the occupants were able to arrange the interior layout to suit
their own tastes – which was welcomed by some as a positive feature but
regretted by others as a time-consuming chore – has to be weighed
against the other characteristics of the Q.M.F., to which we have already
drawn attention: their strength and solidity.

F 6 — You have to know how to arrange it . . . you have to
know how to make the most of it, you see . . .
otherwise the houses are very pleasant . . . *and strong.*

The extent to which the occupant should be allowed to create his own
architectural setting is the subject of certain research projects being carried out at the present time. In this connexion the Pessac experiment
provides some interesting insights into the problems of dwelling houses,
which may well be able to cast light on such enquiries. The principal
difficulty in this kind of investigation is the fact that, by and large,
flexibility, lightness and mobility are difficult to reconcile with the antithetical need for strength and rigidity, qualities which, as I was able to
observe in Pessac, enable new buildings to take root, as it were, and
establish themselves as part of the living environment.

'As far as external
appearances are concerned
the district is a slum area
. . . but from a sociological
point of view it is far from
being a slum area . . .'
M.M. (A Pessac resident).

9
The interviews: spatial and social relations in the district

Individual and collective

Although the nature of the problem changes when considered in town-planning terms, the fundamental antitheses remain the same. Once they had dealt with the question of 'construction games' the members of the group went on to discuss the polarity between liberty and constraint, between mobile and fixed structures, and it was noticeable that their attitudes vacillated continuously, depending on whether they were taking an individual or a collective view.

> s — . . . We were wondering whether, in the final analysis,
> architecture is essentially mobile, essentially flexible,
> in other words something that the householder can
> do something about, or whether it is essentially
> permanent and consequently something that the
> householder can do nothing about . . .

> M — I think you get both these forms. There are things
> the householder can do something about – that
> emerges quite clearly from the enquiries – namely,
> small private houses. There, certainly, the individual
> householder can be allowed a certain latitude as far as
> the interior layout is concerned. But, in my opinion,
> this practice is on the way out.

131

E — But suppose the interior remains the same, where is the difference?

M — The difference is that I would never put a dining-room above a kitchen, if only because of the smells. There's no getting away from the fact that it poses problems. On the other hand, as I have said, there is a possible margin, even in two-storeyed houses. *None the less, in a residential collective a certain amount of authority, a certain amount of regulation has to be accepted; in the present epoch people cannot be left entirely to their own devices, that would be quite impossible.*

E — But what have these people done?

M — It's not that they've done anything, but today you have to be prepared to forgo certain things.

G — And, you know, we're not being deprived all that much, are we? You only need to look at the history of architecture to realize that there have always been police regulations – ever since the fifteenth century, and even before that, in France; I know . . . I can't quote them at length, but they make interesting reading.

M — I'm not trying to defend regulations, I wouldn't like you to think that.

G — No, of course not. I was merely pointing out that these regulations are not something that were introduced the day after the Liberation and had never existed before. Regulations have always existed, ever since the first town-planning project. Consider the height of the buildings along the banks of the Seine, which date from the eighteenth century.

M — *Regulations are appropriate for life in a community, they are not appropriate for architecture.*

G — That's perfectly true . . . There's something I'd like to say at this point; you may not think it very important, but we'll see. When you erect a building, whether it's a small private house or a six-storey block,

there is always an exterior aspect, which is a public
aspect, and an interior aspect, which is a private
aspect. I feel that this needs to be stressed, I think it is
very important.

Our antithetical discussion now seems to have run full circle, for we are
back at the antithesis between the exterior and the interior.

The conceptual thread which links these antithetical ideas has a
spatial equivalent. Thus, although the problems posed by the exterior
of a house are fundamentally different when considered in town-planning terms, when we pass from the private to the public sphere – from
architecture to town planning – we find that the house façades act as a
kind of contact breaker between these two spheres whilst at the same
time ensuring material continuity. It is to this dual function of the urban
cluster – which provides a framework for the collective sphere and a
façade for the private spheres that are to be found in every individual
house – that we must look for an explanation of the present appearance
of the Q.M.F. Although it was conceived by Le Corbusier as a decorative
ensemble the settlement has now become a conglomeration of individual
effects.

The colour schemes that Le Corbusier used – uniform in some cases,
polychromatic in others – were in keeping with his declared intention of
treating external space as a unifying factor, an intention which, incidentally, would seem to be of Cubist provenance. 'We have also applied
a completely new conception of polychromy in pursuit of a purely
architectural objective: using the physical quality of the colours . . .
just as we had used the architectural forms, to shape urban space. This
was an attempt to incorporate architecture into town planning.' It
was also, of course, an attempt to incorporate the individual into the
collective.

But the new colours introduced by the occupants, coupled with the
maintenance work which they carried out, wrought a gradual change.
Instead of helping to stress the collective aspect of the settlement the
buildings assumed the well-defined look of individual family houses.
Thus, the semi-detached villas which initially were difficult to identify
as such were eventually seen for what they were. Moreover, the terraced
houses, which Le Corbusier had painted in a uniform colour so as to
create a continuous façade, now display a succession of completely
individual façades. The collective *composition* conceived by Le Corbusier has been replaced by the *juxtaposition* of individual elements.

We have already encountered the antithesis between the unity of the
Q.M.F. as a 'settlement' – a characteristic which derives from the unity
of Le Corbusier's original conception – and the marked individuality
of the houses in that settlement.

— This place . . . it's *a proper settlement* . . . even though
no two houses are the same: every house has its garden,
but no two houses are aligned in the same way . . . I
repeat that he has built no two houses exactly the same . . .
That's one of his ideas. But it's *still a settlement because
the houses are similar* . . . although not the same: *it is
a settlement because the houses all resemble one another
and were built by the same man. I suppose that is what you
would call a settlement* . . .

s — That means that you have detached houses, individual
houses and a settlement all in one . . .

— Yes, you have, haven't you? And that's what I like about
it here . . .

In this excerpt there is a progression from the antithesis between variety
and standardization to the antithesis between the individual and the
collective. These were dealt with in some detail, it will be remembered,
in my analysis of Le Corbusier's original conception, where I drew
attention to the continuity between these two problems and to the fact
that, in his attempt to reconcile the individual and collective aspects of
the Q.M.F., Le Corbusier used essentially the same kind of approach as
he had adopted to standardization and variety.

The polarity between the individual and the collective appeared in
one form or another in the majority of the interviews and for the most
part was considered to be a positive feature of the settlement: the spatial
balance struck by Le Corbusier between these two poles seems to have
produced a corresponding social balance amongst the occupants:

F 15 — There is a woman who has lived here for fifteen or twenty
years and, although she knows everybody in the district,
she has made no contacts . . . How shall I put it? . . . she
is not over-intimate with people. *She has managed to
preserve her privacy and . . . has none the less remained
friendly with everybody, you know* . . . which is something
you don't find in modern settlements . . . *It's a bit
'block-like'!* . . . the over-all impression, you know . . .
If you look at the road, it's all set out in small blocks . . .
but it also puts you in mind of . . . not of building plots . . .
*Well yes, small houses with gardens, it puts you in mind
of building plots and blocks at one and the same time* . . .
The trees, in the old days, made this district quite
charming . . . it looked a bit . . . a bit suburban . . . The

134

good thing about this kind of district is that although . . .
*the houses are set close together . . . we still retain a
certain individuality,* which you don't get in modern
blocks, for example . . . I lived for a long time in the
settlement at Camponnac, which is considered to be a
settlement of some standing, and I found that it was not
only extremely friendly, you know, which meant that . . .
although your neighbours were . . . well, there were
people from various social classes . . . you have very
friendly contacts *and yet you are never disturbed as you
are in a block or even in some settlements where the houses
are set close together,* I don't quite know why that is . . .
Perhaps because it's been there for some time, people
have established certain patterns of behaviour . . .
patterns of behaviour or perhaps you could call it a
tradition[1] . . . and yet, although the houses are either
semi-detached or terraced, you are never troubled by
your neighbours . . . quite apart from the large blocks
there are also settlements where the houses are well
spaced out but where the people busy themselves with
gossip, whereas here, I've lived here for some time now
and I know the people. Perhaps, it's due partly to the
layout, the houses are aligned on roads; and then, the
way it's broken up, it's more or less T-shaped, perhaps
that's why, I wonder . . . but you certainly have the
impression that, when you're at home, you really are at
home . . .

The external aspect of the Q.M.F. derives primarily from its function as
a settlement.

a — What is a settlement?

OF 33 — Well . . . this *group* of houses, I suppose . . .

And a further comment on the external aspect of the district by a
second outsider:

OF 35 — The way they're massed, packed together, like that, I
find that unaesthetic . . . the fact that they're arranged
like that, *as a settlement,* they could have been set out
differently, although I still wouldn't like them . . . I

[1] See footnote on p.136.

135

don't like settlements, I don't like ensembles, I don't
like anything of that kind! . . . A flat stuck in the middle
of the countryside like that! . . . To have a flat in a town
is quite different from having a flat like that, stuck in the
middle of the countryside . . . Like that, you have all
the inconvenience of living in a flat and all the inconvenience of living in a suburb . . . [*in other words, lack of
services, shops, leisure activities and so on* . . .]

We now encounter yet another resident whose ideas were determined
partly by a stereotyped image and partly by his own personal experience.
This interviewee told us that he had recently read Jane Jacobs's book,
The Death and Life of Great American Cities, with great interest, which
would explain his apparent preference for 'real towns'.

M 19 — He was a town planner and, like many town planners,
was opposed to towns . . . to be perfectly frank, I prefer
a town, a real town . . . I don't mind the country . . . but
a suburb, to my mind, is neither town nor country, it's
a sort of magma . . . of course within this magma you
find many different solutions, and the one I like best is
the one we have here, the garden city . . .

This same interviewee then went on to express a number of opinions
about the Pessac settlement, which would suggest that he was really
very favourably disposed towards it:

— There is a certain density here, and yet people don't
have the feeling that they're living on top of one another
. . . the children can play outside, and yet their mothers
can still keep an eye on them.

This person also admitted to a 'very powerful sense of belonging' which
in his opinion was typical of all the residents.[2]

Finally, this interviewee, who is at present a tenant, is thinking very
seriously of buying his house. The contradiction between his statements
and his behaviour could not be more clearly demonstrated.

[2] This 'sense of belonging' would tie up with the 'tradition' mentioned by F 15 on
p.135. Clearly, there is a strong community sense in the Q.M.F.

We have seen that by and large the occupants commented favourably on their district. But there is one fundamental point that has to be established in this connexion: the people whose views we have quoted and who, in one way or another, volunteered an opinion on the district, all lived in the heart of the Q.M.F. This observation, which was first made in the course of the initial enquiry, needs to be correlated with a second observation concerning a certain marginal zone, which revealed quite a remarkable degree of social cohesion.

But let me first outline the topography of the district. Coming from the centre of Pessac the visitor approaches the Q.M.F. by the Avenue Frugès, which skirts the settlement on one side but does not enter it. A second road, the Rue Le Corbusier, runs more or less through the middle of the district and is flanked by houses on either side. The third and last road, the Allée des Arcades, is an internal cul-de-sac with central access from the Avenue Frugès.

The first point to be noted is that the zones created by the road network did not correspond to the sociological zones which we were able to observe (and whose social cohesion varied from zone to zone). Far from being segregated by the roads, these sociological zones were centred on them. Thus, instead of having a divisive effect, the roads provide a means of contact for the people living on either side. Incidentally, there is virtually no risk of road accidents since there is no through traffic.

One surprising feature is the fact that the sociological zones centred on the various roads *have not been influenced in any way* by the diversity of the architecture. For example, the Rue Le Corbusier is flanked on one side by two-storeyed terraced villas and on the other by three-storeyed semi-detached 'skyscrapers', whose alignment and spacing are quite irregular. And yet good neighbourly relations exist between householders on both sides of the road.

The Avenue Frugès provides an even more striking example of this kind of development. There, where Le Corbusier's terraced houses face a row of typical suburban villas on the other side of the road, close neighbourly relations have even led to marriage in certain cases.

> **M 2** — *That row over there* . . . but, of course, it's always been like that . . . and, you know, people are a bit envious of us because we get on so well with one another . . . if someone needs a helping hand . . . that's it! Everybody goes to see what they can do . . . if someone is taken ill in the night . . . everybody goes to ask if they can help . . .

NF 27 — That . . . is our *fief* . . . once, on July 14, my neighbour
fixed up a record player, and we all danced in the street
. . .

One lady had had her house built facing away from the road, which
her neighbours – significantly enough – had found surprising:

— My neighbours asked me: – *Why didn't you have your
house built overlooking the road?* – I told them that I
preferred a southern aspect . . .

M 1 — You know, *this road here* compared with *the road round
the back*, well I think it's more pleasant . . . of course,
there aren't many of us . . . and it's been . . . well . . .
kept in fairly good repair . . . but the road round the
back, really it's not very pleasant . . . the left-hand side
especially, the big houses . . .

F 6 — *On this road* the people are very well behaved, very
correct, and you know there's a pleasant atmosphere . . .
round the back? No, I don't go round there . . . Apart
from Mme B, I don't know very many people there . . . I
never go round there . . . there's nothing to interest me
. . . I find it's better at home . . . people make their own
little lives for themselves . . . Here, everyone stays at
home, but of course if . . . someone is in trouble . . .
people show their solidarity.

a — You know M. and Mme B *on the other road*?

— The Bs are charming people. But *it's not the same*, you're
more . . . because . . . when you go out, it's usually on
this road, not that one . . .

a — And this road? . . .

M 3 — Oh, it's very good . . . it's very good here. Because, you
see, on this road, since there are only one, two, three,
four, five – only seven of us in all, *we've always got on
very well* . . . everybody, you know, it's quiet, peaceful,
whereas over there, round the back, there are far more
people, it's a road with houses on both sides, and then
there are those semis, the big houses; you have . . . a
tenant in front of you and a tenant behind you, so there

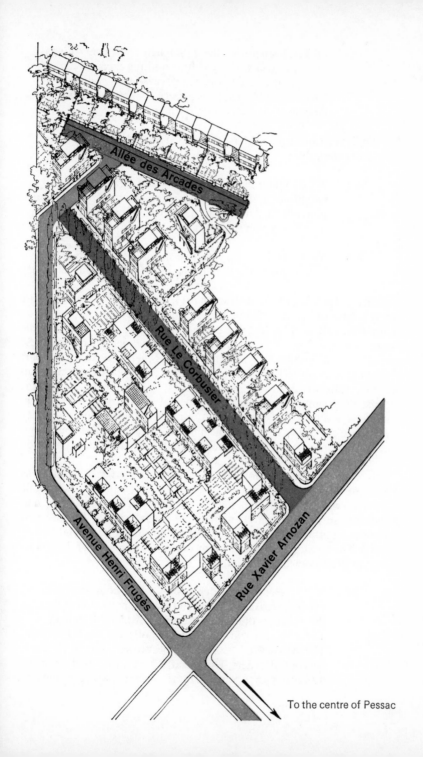

Allée des Arcades

Rue Le Corbusier

Avenue Henri Frugès

Rue Xavier Arnozan

To the centre of Pessac

are far more houses there than here; here everything is
quiet . . . you know, you hear nothing except the trains,
and you get used to them; *otherwise everybody is very
quiet, very pleasant, people know one another, help one
another if the need arises, it's fine . . .*

The family relationships that have developed on and around this road
are quite remarkable:

M 2 — My daughter married the son of our right-hand
neighbour and is now living round the back . . . My son
married the daughter of our left-hand neighbour and is
now living over there, on the other side of the road . . .

F 3 — My sister lives opposite, and she bought the house next
to ours for our children, who used to live in it at one time.

A glance at the plan of the district on p.142 shows how close knit these
family relationships were. Similar relationships developed in other parts
of the Q.M.F., it is true, but not on the same scale as on the Avenue
Frugès. On the face of it, one is very much inclined to regard these
particular relationships as symptomatic of a general desire on the part
of the people living on this road to entrench themselves in their marginal
position, thus dissociating themselves, as it were, from the Q.M.F.
Because the Avenue Frugès was the principal access route to the settlement these seven houses were the first thing most people saw when they
approached the Q.M.F. They were the most marginal of all the houses and
would, therefore, have tended to promote an isolationist attitude
(' . . . round the back? no, I don't go round there . . .').

This 'exclusive' zone, whose occupants seemed perfectly happy, was
in marked contrast to a second zone, which was equally remarkable
in its own way. This was situated in the heart of the settlement and
revealed a surprisingly large number of social misfits (depressives,
alcoholics, neurotics, successful and attempted suicide cases and homo-
sexuals). These cases were described by one of the residents of the Q.M.F.,
an impartial and objective observer:

M — X is subject to fits of depression, which come over him
when the seasons change and make him so violent that
the members of his family are in considerable danger.
The woman at No. . . . is an alcoholic, her son is in prison.
The man at No. . . . is also subject to serious and violent
nervous disorders. The son at No. . . ., who died when he
was about forty, was not quite normal. Two years ago an

old man committed suicide at No. . . . The old woman at No. . . is half mad, she has made one suicide attempt, she is always picking quarrels, usually with the man in the house opposite, she is feared in the district, she'd report you to the police as soon as look at you; as for her husband, he's been banned from the district and could well be in prison. At No. . . . the son is more or less openly homosexual, and his parents turn a blind eye . . . all these cases are so obvious, you can't help noticing them . . . I don't think it's the district that has produced them, I think they're the sort of thing you tend to find in any poor district. But these social misfits have become well integrated here; despite their problems, all these people manage to live together in a reasonably satisfactory way. Those who want to keep to themselves do so, those who want to live in one another's pocket do so. The only source of discord is the family at No. . . . But if all these people were cooped up in a high rise building, I imagine it would be pretty hellish. In my opinion, the great thing about this district is that it has a density that is high enough to prevent people from feeling isolated and low enough to ensure that they don't live on top of one another . . . it's easy for the mothers to keep an eye on their children, the neighbours form a natural extension of the family; and as for the adults, there is a great deal of tolerance, people are accepted for what they are . . . Of course, all these observations apply only to this particular sector: there is an invisible barrier between this sector and the rest of the Rue Le Corbusier, our neighbours in the house opposite are always saying that they couldn't live on the Rue Le Corbusier because 'the people there never stop fighting . . .'

What strikes us here is the way in which the social conditions found in the district reflect its spatial organization. We see that the antithesis between interior and exterior, whose significance has already been established at an architectural level, is also relevant at an urban level. The fact of the matter is that the district is composed of three distinct zones: a marginal zone, in which social contacts are friendly and, in certain cases, have led to family ties; a neutral zone, in which everything seems 'normal'; and an interior zone, in which we find numerous psycho-social problems. Later, on page 147, we shall see that there is also a definite link between the siting of individual houses in the district and the psychological and social characteristics of their occupants.

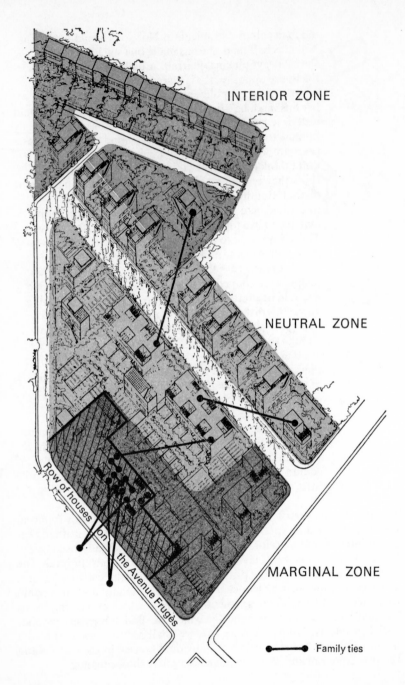

INTERIOR ZONE

NEUTRAL ZONE

MARGINAL ZONE

Row of houses on the Avenue Frugès

Family ties

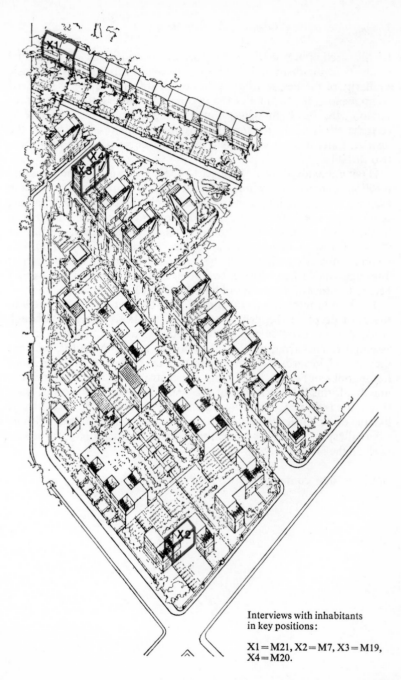

Interviews with inhabitants
in key positions:

X1 = M21, X2 = M7, X3 = M19,
X4 = M20.

143

In this section we shall be considering the positions of individual residents in the district. The *constant* factor in this study is the basic similarity of the Pessac villas, which resulted from the use of standard components. Like the first of the two *variable* factors, namely the conversions, this has been analysed in an earlier chapter. We now have to consider the second *variable*—the positions of the residents within the district. Later I shall show that there is a correlation between these two variables.

Having already drawn attention to the significance of the marginal position occupied by a whole group of houses, I now propose to quote excerpts from two interviews, each of which is concerned with one particular house. The first of these (**M 7**) refers to the second house seen by the visitor when he arrives in the settlement. Since the first is part of the small row of houses on the Avenue Frugès (see **F 6**, p.138), this second house is clearly one of the most isolated in the whole district: although sandwiched between two other houses it does not and cannot belong to either of the groups of houses to which these belong.

The second interview from which I shall be quoting (**M 21**) refers to the most deeply embedded house in the whole settlement. Although situated at the extreme end of the Allée des Arcades, it differs in one essential respect from all the other houses on the Allée for, whereas they all look inwards towards the centre of the settlement, this particular house looks outwards, away from the centre and towards the railway line that forms the outer limit of the Q.M.F. The view of the Q.M.F. from this house is, in fact, cut off by a clump of high trees and consequently, like the other house mentioned above, it is very much isolated. With its external aspect and its end position it seems almost to have turned its back on the district.

But let us now compare the two interviews:

M 7 — If I were to tell you that I don't even know three-quarters of the district . . . in the first place people like us, we have jobs which keep us away most of the day . . . but one thing I can tell you, the district is quiet . . .

s — But what is the district exactly?

— Well, you know, the district . . . as I've already told you, I don't know it very well, for very good reasons, because with the sort of jobs we do, we set out in the mornings and come home at night, or else we might be on night shift, and then I go to bed as soon as I get home, so I couldn't even tell you the names of the other roads or the people's names; sometimes when visitors ask me where so and so lives, I always send them on to someone else who knows more about the district . . . My immediate neighbours . . . well, of course, I know them . . . but, otherwise . . . we work most of the time, more's the pity, because when you're on nights, you sleep all day . . . that's the way things are, you know . . . but, of course . . . if someone needs a helping hand . . . there was one neighbour of ours . . . one day – she had a little boy . . . who'd had an accident, and that's how we got to know her, because I had the car there, so I fetched the car straight away . . . you know . . . But, you see . . . it was only because there was a reason!

M 21 — Well, the people who live opposite . . . well . . . there was an occasion once when I helped them with something and since then, of course, they've spoken to me . . . and of course I've spoken to them . . . but apart from that . . . that's all, that's as far as it went . . . but then what do you expect . . . I set out early in the mornings, I start work at 7.30 am, so does my wife, I have my lunch where I work, and then I come home in the evening . . . but you come home, you close the front door, and that's that . . . you know . . . which means that basically . . . I don't know anybody . . . it could hardly be otherwise . . . but *don't think I'm complaining about the district*! . . . I have nothing to complain about . . . well, you know . . . I have the woods at the side of the house, I have shade, I have the little courtyard, the garden, I have a garage . . . I'm very well off, I have peace and quiet . . . *the house is comfortable* . . .

Here we find closely parallel views expressed by two residents, both of whom live in marginal positions. The first of these two interviewees went on to say:

M 7 — But if you want to have people in, well you can't, with the best will in the world, you just can't do it. You know, we finish work pretty late in the evenings . . . and when I'm on 'lates' I like to lie in a bit the next day; very soon now I'll be off to work and I'll not be back till 8 o'clock this evening, yet tomorrow, although it's Sunday, I'll be starting again at 5 o'clock . . . and working through till midday. So you see, I'm never in the district . . . that's the way things are . . .

s — If I understand you correctly, it is . . . it is due to the nature of your work, or rather to your hours of work, that you occupy this special . . . and somewhat unintegrated position in the community . . .

— Yes, that's right, that's the reason . . .

s — But what is the community? . . .

— Well, it's all the occupants, all those who live in the district . . . obviously, I suppose, one could make contacts . . . but I'm not so sure, you know . . . I tell you . . . it's something I've never thought about because . . . the question just didn't arise for me . . . you have to . . . to take things as they come . . . that's all you can do, isn't it . . . later on you try . . . you might try to organize something but, you know, the situation being what it is . . . in this particular sphere at least . . . there's not much . . . there are so many . . . so many other things that need to be improved and claim your attention that . . . that . . . how . . . can you try . . . why should you try, you know, to discuss matters with . . . well, with your neighbours . . . in this way . . . all right, so you go and see them, but then you might go four or five days or ten days . . . or even fourteen days . . . without seeing them again . . . no! that's the way things are . . . in this particular sphere at least . . . that's the way things are . . . you have to fight hard enough for things like wage increases without bothering your head about whether you should . . . improve your relations with your

146

neighbours, especially since . . . it's not the easiest thing in the world to do . . . and, anyway, is there any need for improvement? . . . we get on with everybody as it is, you know . . . if somebody does you a service, you repay them . . . automatically; but above all . . . it often happens that . . . that you can't make contact with anybody [*awkward working hours*] . . . once you find yourself in that kind of situation you can't have personal relations with your neighbours . . . that's the plain truth of the matter . . .

The correlation that I was able to establish in these two cases between the personalities and behaviour patterns of the occupants on the one hand and the position of their houses on the other was also indicated by two other interviews. Here too the interviewees lived in houses which occupied virtually identical positions.

The first of these two was the person who took such a keen interest in sociology and who had suggested that a sociological enquiry into the development of the Q.M.F. might prove a very interesting experiment. He lived in a semi-detached house at the far end of the Avenue Frugès, a position which is so exposed that, to newcomers to the district, his house seems to stand out almost like an observation post. Not surprisingly, therefore, it impressed itself forcibly both on myself and on my collaborator during our frequent visits to the district. On numerous occasions we also saw one or other of the occupants going from one room to another and looking out of the window as they passed. This was subsequently explained to us when we interviewed the owner:

M 19 — These walls have eyes, a fact which enables the occupants to exercise a certain control: the neighbours can keep an eye on the children . . . that helps to create a spirit of co-operation . . . any stranger entering the district is recognized at once . . .

The position occupied by this house – at the intersection of the three roads which serve the Q.M.F. – matches the personality, or rather the interests, of its occupant in what is surely quite a remarkable manner. This man, who is so interested in sociology, lives in a house that provides him with what is virtually an observation post, from which he is able to maintain the social control to which he referred but which he clearly implied was being exercised by others. Moreover, when he said that the 'neighbours can keep an eye on the children' he was again imputing his own actions to other people, for he subsequently stated that *he himself* had intervened in the children's quarrels on the bit of ground

147

situated in front of his study and in the heart of the settlement, which served as a playground.

This subjectivity, which might perhaps be described as 'positional' subjectivity, was displayed quite openly when the interviewee suggested that 'the isolation of the district is not a retreat' . . . It so happens that, although it is situated in the heart of the settlement, his particular house enjoys a distant view of the countryside beyond the railway line and consequently is not boxed in in the same way as the other houses in the same zone. In making this statement therefore, the interviewee was quite clearly applying to the whole of the district an assessment which had been prompted by his own house alone. And if we compare this observation with the observation made in an earlier chapter in connection with the same interviewee concerning the essential duality of houses – as objects of intellectual analysis on the one hand and as containers in which people live their lives on the other – we find that, in this particular instance, the occupant was in fact confusing architectural and town-planning values.

Of course, the reader might also feel inclined to question the validity of this interpretation – in architectural, not sociological terms – and to reject it as subjective. But before doing so I must ask him to consider the following antithetical case, which also illustrates my argument.

What we are concerned with in this case is not so much the district as the architectural quality of a particular house and the close personal relationship that the occupant has developed to that house. But, although this interviewee scarcely mentioned the *district as such* in the whole course of his interview, his observations are, I believe, none the less relevant to our present purpose. In fact, I find this omission extremely significant.

When I called on him I discovered that he was building a sailing boat in his spare time:

> **M 20** — Yes, it will be finished by June; I'll make a cruise then, to the Canaries or perhaps even further afield . . . *I want to get away from it all* . . .

> — You'll leave your wife and children behind? . . . Your wife isn't interested in that sort of thing? . . .

> — Not in the slightest . . . as for the children, I'd be risking their lives, *and anyway the boat has been designed for a single person* . . . . . .

a — And you're building it yourself . . .

— *Everybody wants to build a boat of his own . . .* but as far as I know there are very few in France . . . *in my profession I am obliged to talk to other people . . .*

This interviewee is the next door neighbour of the 'sociologist' whom we have just been discussing; they live in adjoining semi-detached houses. The difference in temperament between the 'sociologist', an extremely affable man who takes a keen interest in social problems and relationships within the settlement, and the 'sailor', a man with a great longing for solitude who regards social ralationships as a necessary duty, could hardly be more pronounced. And their semi-detached houses, which occupy virtually the same position but face in opposite directions, aptly reflect their antithetical attitudes. We have already seen, moreover, that although they are situated in the heart of the settlement, these particular houses enjoy a view of the surrounding countryside, which means that they too reveal antithetical characteristics. We also find that this occupant, who was so averse to social contact, was able to reach his house without passing through the settlement:

M 20 — The district . . . I always drive past very quickly in my car, I never look at it, I always go along the Avenue Frugès.

. . . The Avenue Frugès it will be remembered, merely flanks the Q.M.F. And once he had reached his house in the heart of the settlement (which, since it was built as a cul-de-sac, constitutes 'a more enclosed world than other settlements') the occupant was completely sheltered.

But in his case the actual house was more important than the district. We have seen that Le Corbusier drew much of his inspiration from steamship design and, in point of fact, his Pessac houses were very much like ships, a fact commented on by several of the residents and one that was clearly of considerable significance to this particular occupant. The interior of his house had a neat, trim look about it, due to the discreet combination of solid wood and veneered furniture with decorative objects such as ropes, sea charts and a buoy. Once on board his ship he evidently felt more at ease and no longer needed to insulate himself, for at home he proposed to create the maximum amount of open space by removing all the partitions:

a— What are your plans? . . .

M 20 — Here I've already removed one partition . . . it wasn't very good. I don't know whether it was original or whether my predecessor had it built [*in actual fact, the occupant was reverting to Le Corbusier's open plan design*] . . . but it took up space needed for other purposes, prevented the air from circulating, prevented light from entering the house, prevented the heat from rising . . . so, in the end, I removed it . . .

Later, when he was showing me over the house, the occupant told me about further modifications that he was going to make:

> **M 20** — Now here . . . this partition comes out, so does that one . . . and here, this partition and that one . . . both out . . . it will create more space . . . *so that it won't be so shut off* . . .

This occupant also intends to do away with the concrete parapet on the outside staircase:

> **M 20** — I can then install a cast iron ramp . . . which will have an aesthetic effect, since it will be, well . . .
>
> **a** — Since it will be transparent? . . .
>
> — Exactly! Since it will be transparent . . .

This occupant – who, as we have seen, lives a secluded life – knew nothing about the history of the Q.M.F. project and had not even heard of Le Corbusier. But he regarded his house as a veritable dream house: since it fulfilled all his requirements it provided him with a container which afforded protection from the elements and in which he could create any interior arrangement he wished by the use of moveable screens. As a result, he now has what is virtually a Japanese house – but a Japanese house with extremely solid walls.

Not surprisingly, he bought his house without a moment's hesitation:

> **M 20** — From an aesthetic point of view . . . I didn't like it, especially the outside . . . but I saw its potential immediately . . .

I was surprised to hear that the villa had held no aesthetic appeal for him and commented on this. I was then told:

M 20 — These houses, they were a bit too much like a . . .
steamship for my liking . . . .

  a — And yet you seem to like ships . . .

    — Yes, that's true, but we distinguish at sea between
steam and sail; there has always been bad feeling
between the men on sailing ships and the men on
steamships; they can't stand the sight of one another . . .

It is in his rejection of steamship design that the occupant parts company with Le Corbusier. It seems hardly likely that he could have endured the far more regimented life led by the residents of the *Cité Radieuse* in Marseille. But in his family house in Pessac he is perfectly content because there he is free to do as he pleases:

    — It's the sort of house where you could introduce all
manner of combinations.

Although this occupant lives in a secluded house in a secluded district he has none the less contrived to create even greater seclusion for himself by erecting a structure on the terrace rather like a commander's turret on a ship, to which he is able to retire whenever he feels the need.

This chapter is, of course, concerned primarily with the district as an entity, but it was important that this brief analysis, in which I have dealt with the attitude of one particular occupant to Le Corbusier's architectural conception, should have been included in it. It is in any case quite impossible to place architectural and town-planning questions in completely separate compartments, for we have already seen in an earlier chapter that they are intimately connected with one another. And now, in this last interview, we have encountered a person whose total lack of interest in any questions touching upon the district – but especially social questions – seems to be closely linked with his attitude to the architectural quality of his own house.

Finally – and this was the principal reason for including this analysis in the present chapter – we have to consider the *antithesis* between the temperaments of the 'sociologist' and the 'sailor' and the fact that this has not prevented them from living harmoniously in adjoining houses. Indeed, their respective families are on the best of terms with one another.

The positions occupied by different houses in the district and the conversions

We have already noted the significance of the positions occupied by different houses in the district and, in view of this, it seemed desirable to try to establish whether there was any sort of relationship between these positions and the conversions carried out by so many of the occupants.

The most obvious hypothesis was that the external conversions constituted a reaction to the use of standardized building components. This of course would have presupposed that the occupants wanted to *personalize* their homes which, as we have already discovered from the group discussion, has been widely assumed. On this basis it seemed reasonable to expect that the nature of the conversions would be determined to a considerable extent by the positions of the houses in the settlement, in other words that the more impersonal a particular house was, the more extensive the conversions would be.

Subsequently I was able to demonstrate a correlation between these two factors. But the result was the exact opposite of what I had anticipated. Although it is not possible to provide exact statistics covering all fifty-one houses in the settlement, I did discover that wherever particularly striking conversions had been carried out, the houses in question and more especially the positions they occupied, were far from impersonal. Thus, the conversions would seem to have been effected, not – as I had assumed – in order to personalise the standardized appearance of the houses, but in order to bring out or enhance the personal qualities that they already possessed. It will be remembered in this connexion that the original occupants of the Q.M.F. did not object to the standardization employed by Le Corbusier, a fact which would tend to confirm this thesis.

In order to demonstrate the correlation between the sites occupied by certain houses and the external conversions effected by their occupants I have produced a diagram (p.156) featuring the different groups of houses: by using certain criteria – type of house, number of storeys, access route, position of main façade (facing the road or facing away from the road) – we are able to represent certain groups of houses which intersect at specific points. In this diagram the houses situated at the intersections belong to various groups and consequently are more distinctive than those which belong to only one group; and it was in these more distinctive houses that I observed the most striking conversions.

This thesis is, of course, based not only on my own observations but also on the observations made by the occupants in the course of the interviews. One interesting point is the fact that in certain key positions the occupants paid particular attention to vegetation with the result

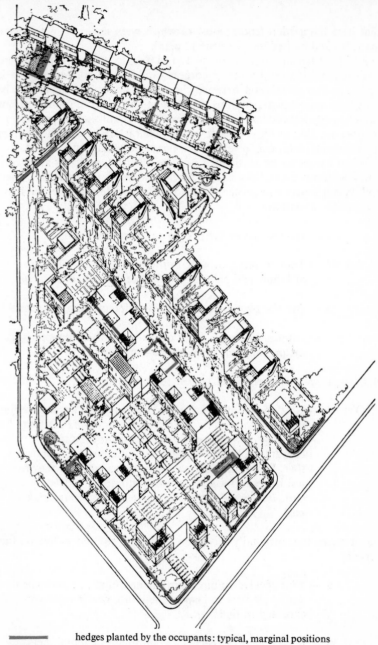

hedges planted by the occupants: typical, marginal positions

trees trained by the occupants: typical, marginal positions

old wooden fences: internal

façades painted in the original colours: internal and central

153

that here the garden fences, most of which were made of metal, were often backed by hedges (see general plan).

As in settlements elsewhere, so too in Pessac, the most prominent positions of all were the street corners; and in this connexion one is struck by the correlation between the spatial and what might best be called the sociological positions: it is almost invariably in such positions (which, as we have already seen, may well reflect antithetical properties) that we are able to observe both asocial characteristics on the part of the occupants and, conversely, the appearance of catalytic agents.

When I went to the settlement of Pape Clément, which is situated a few kilometres from Pessac, to interview some of the residents, their ambivalent attitude to corner sites and to the people who lived on them was readily apparent:

a — Do you know the people *on the corner*?

OF 32 — They're very . . . well, in the first place they're never at home, and anyway , . . they're *not all that sociable* . . .

a — Are the people on the corner different from the others?

— Oh yes, although . . . it depends on which people you mean, some of them are more or less . . .

But the *people on the corner* also *want* to be different:

OM 30 — Now the paintwork [*on the balcony*], you know, I redid it the way it was . . . in the original colours . . . but *the chap on the corner*, he didn't want the same colours, he had to be different; of course, I suppose that, like that, when people come to see him, they're not likely to miss his house, you know . . . [*the occupant on the corner has painted his balcony bright red*].

But it seems that originally this interviewee also wanted to live on the corner:

a — You decided to buy from the brochure . . . and when you came here to inspect the house was it what you expected to find? . . .

OM 30 — It was what I expected . . . although in actual fact . . . I would have preferred an end house, you know . . .

but I couldn't get an end house . . . so I had to take this one . . . ideally, of course, I'd like a detached house . . .

This interviewee lives in a terraced house on the edge of the settlement and, like the Pessac residents who lived in marginal positions, was happy to do so:

OM 30 — It's better here than in the centre of the settlement. You see, there's nobody living opposite, there's just an empty space and then the vineyards . . . you feel a little . . . more secluded . . . and, you see, I always liked to be independent . . .

Curiously enough, although this occupant does not intend to carry out any conversions (see p.119), he would have considered doing so if he had had an end-of-terrace house:

— If I had had an end house . . . I might have tried to do something about the garage. Turn it into an extra room; some people have done that.

Another occupant whom we interviewed in the settlement of Pape Clément was positively hypersociable: after failing to obtain an end-of-terrace house on the edge of the settlement she settled for an end-of-terrace house in the heart of the settlement:

OF 32 — We've formed a little group . . . we often take our apéritif together . . . or share a late meal, I've had some good times with my little group of neighbours . . . thinking about it, I'd say that . . . *it all came about through me* . . . it's a question of what you're used to, you know . . . I'm used to a little clan . . .

a — So really you have acted as a catalyst for your neighbours . . .

— Yes . . . yes, something of that sort . . .

In Pessac I was able to observe that the people whom we interviewed as well as those who declined to be interviewed were influenced in their attitude towards us – my colleague and I were, of course, outsiders – by the position of their houses in the settlement. It is, after all, surely significant that those who refused to co-operate lived in the heart of the cluster whilst those who were the most communicative lived in equally prominent positions elsewhere. Moreover, if we consider the different groups of houses (see diagram on p.61), we find that in the interviews conducted on one of the terraced rows there seems to have been genuine contact whilst on the second terraced row there was only limited contact in all but the last two houses (Nos.19 and 20). On the third terraced row we were able to establish genuine contact with only one person, the occupant of the end house (No.21). The houses with the least modifications – and the only ones to have retained their original colours – are situated in the middle of the internal terraced rows, a fact which I also find significant. As for the houses at the entrance to the settlement, they resemble the houses at the rear in so far as they look as if they don't really belong:

M 8 — Those houses over there don't seem to belong to the settlement, *they look as if they were put there just to round it off . . .*

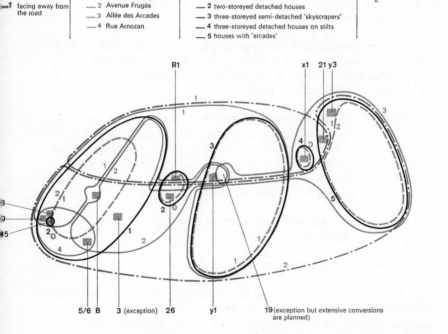

facing the road	—1 Rue Le Corbusier	—1 two-storeyed terraced houses	$\frac{1}{2}$ No. of neighbours
facing away from the road	—2 Avenue Frugès	—2 two-storeyed detached houses	
	—3 Allée des Arcades	—3 three-storeyed semi-detached 'skyscrapers'	
	—4 Rue Arnozan	—4 three-storeyed detached houses on stilts	
		—5 houses with 'arcades'	

Diagram showing the different groups of houses and the individual houses at their intersections which have been extensively converted.

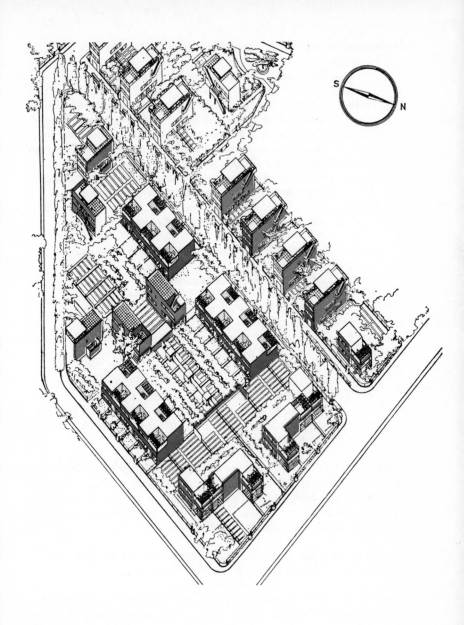

Quartiers Modernes Frugès
at Pessac near Bordeaux, showing
the original colour scheme.

157

Once again we see the importance of the positional factor.

> **a** — Your house is situated at the corner . . .

> **F 10** — Which is very pleasant [*the interviewee responded without hesitation*], but unfortunately it is very damp, that's the only drawback, the damp . . . but then you can't have everything . . . If I owned it, I'd have a roof built [*According to my thesis this house should have been converted: we now see why it was not and that it might possibly be converted at some future date*] . . .

> — *You know, with a nice roof front and back,* but unfortunately I am not the owner; it's a great pity *because this house would lend itself to conversion.*

> **a** — Why this house in particular?

> — *Because it's on a corner* . . .

And, in fact, an occupant who lived on another corner had made extensive alterations to her house:

> **F 6** — Once we'd got everything done it was the prettiest house in the district . . . there used to be metal shutters because it was used as a grocer's and general store, a corner shop . . . I took it on the spot, I didn't waste time looking at other houses.

But there were two other houses which also seemed to contradict my thesis. In the first of these, which occupied a corner position and where I would have expected to find extensive outside modifications, no significant alterations had been made. However, the occupant assured me that he intended to change the façade:

> **M 15** — If you come back next year you won't recognize the place, it will be completely different . . .

The principal alteration which he had in mind was the addition of an outside staircase leading to the terrace. But, quite apart from these projected changes, there was already one unusual feature about the house at the time of my visit, which lent some support to my ideas: a magnificent tree was growing at the corner of the house, its branches twined around the stilt and its crown on a level with the terrace.

158

Clearly, this highly ornamental feature had been introduced in order to demonstrate that this was a corner house.

The contradiction implied by the second of these two houses was of a different order. Here extensive modifications had been carried out (see illustration 67) despite the fact that the position of the house was perfectly ordinary except in so far as it belonged to the marginal row of houses on the Avenue Frugès. I eventually learnt that the house had been converted when one of the owner's children had made his first communion. In this particular case, therefore, the conversions were prompted not by the positional significance of the house but by the temporal significance of a special event in the lives of its occupants.

To my mind the most important aspect of this correlation between the positions and the individuality of the Pessac houses is the fact that it demonstrates the relationship between the kind of form that we are able to impose on urban space and the reactions and behaviour patterns of the residents. Thus, there is a specific relationship between urban space and urban dwellers at a collective level.

On a number of occasions the people living in the Q.M.F. referred to the educational value of different kinds of dwelling place in terms of communal living:

> OM 26 — Here everybody has tried to express his personality . . .
> but we have to learn to live in a community . . . I live
> in a villa in a Paris suburb, and my children are far
> too independent . . . they're not learning how to live
> in a community . . .
>
> a — You think that people's personalities are formed by
> the places they live in . . .
>
> — Yes, I believe they are . . . people will have to be
> taught what a community is because it is communities
> that are productive . . . and communities are found in
> towns . . . a suburb like this is fine for people who've
> retired . . . but it's in the towns that people work . . .

Here again we see the close links which exist between social and architectural space.

'It is useless to try to describe the things that one sees, for visual objects can never be expressed in words; and it is useless to try to make people see – by means of images, metaphors or comparisons – the ideas that one is in the process of expressing, for the sphere in which they shine forth is not the sphere revealed by the eyes but that defined by syntactical sequences . . .'   M. Foucault

Conclusion

Apart from providing a monograph on the Pessac project this study has enabled me to shed some light on the problems of standardization, functionalism and architectural semiotics, with which architects and town planners are now having to contend on a wide scale. It has also drawn attention to certain new problems, which might best be described as 'toposociological' and which clearly call for further investigation. Because of its place in the history of architecture, because of the personality of its creator and the goal which he had set himself, the Pessac project lent itself particularly well to the analysis of such problems. By now some forty years have passed since Le Corbusier built his workers' settlement. But the questions which he asked himself then are still being asked today, and in much the same form.

Certain aspects of the Pessac development have now been clarified. In the first place we have seen that the Q.M.F. were not an 'architectural failure': the modifications carried out by the occupants constitute a positive and not a negative consequence of Le Corbusier's original conception. Pessac could only be regarded as a failure if it had failed to satisfy the needs of the occupants. In point of fact, however, it not only allowed the occupants sufficient latitude to satisfy their needs, by doing so it also helped them to realize what those needs were. Because of the individuality of certain houses in the district – and it was in these that the most extensive conversions were carried out – the district itself acquired a highly individual character. It is, in fact, a small world in itself, closed and open at one and the same time and imbued with an individuality that I was privileged to study. On the other hand, there were certain zones in the settlement where the houses were far more impersonal with the result that they were converted to a much lesser extent; this merely goes to show that, in certain circumstances, a settlement is more likely to inhibit individuality than encourage it. The dwellings in Maine–Montparnasse are doubtless less susceptible to conversion than the Pessac houses, and it is improbable that they will ever be embellished with frontons or baskets of flowers. But this only means that the architectural failure of Maine–Montparnasse is likely to pass unnoticed . . .

But, of course, Le Corbusier built other things besides the Q.M.F. In his *unités d'habitation* the balance between the individual and the collective – in so far as it exists – will have been struck in a different way. And in this connexion we might well ask ourselves whether the 'failure of Pessac' – which is how Le Corbusier regarded this project – influenced his later designs.

Of course, what Le Corbusier *said* and what he *did* were often two different things. For the architect, as for the artist, it is not enough to do a thing, he also has to see what he has done. That is what really matters. The duality of these two actions was clearly expressed by Le Corbusier: 'You must always say what you see and, what is more, you must see what you see.'

The importance which he attached to seeing things is understandable for, where the architect is concerned, looking at things, seeing things, is in itself an action.

Ordinary people, on the other hand, do not spend their lives looking at their houses, they are more concerned with living in them. And in 1959, when a critic of architecture recalled his visit to Pessac, he wrote: 'Sitting in a garden on the roof of one of the houses, in the shade of a leafy maple tree, I could see how the sun dappled the Havana-brown wall with blobs of light. The only purpose of the wall was to frame the view. The buildings opposite could be perceived as houses only with great difficulty. The one to the left was simply a light-green plane without cornice or gutter. An oblong hole was cut out of the plane exactly like the one I was looking through. Behind and to the right of the green house were row-houses with coffee-brown façades and cream-coloured sides and behind them rose the tops of blue "sky-scrapers".'[1]

With his sculptural attitude to the urban scene this critic is clearly poles apart from the occupants and no doubt even further removed from Le Corbusier.

Le Corbusier's genius stemmed in no small measure from his realization that an architect must not only *do* things but also *say* things. This insight is demonstrated by the many phrases which he coined and which

---

[1] Steen Eiler Rasmussen, *Experiencing Architecture* (Cambridge, 1959), p.95.

appear in his numerous and invaluable writings: *cité radieuse, unité d'habitation, usine verte, immeuble-villa, maison-outil, machine à habiter* and so on.

Admittedly, Le Corbusier was not the only architect to realize that things have to be said. But he was perhaps exceptional in that, although he *said* a great deal, he also *did* a great deal. His works are there to prove it. And then there is his mother's famous dictum, which tells us so much about him but which would have been quite meaningless if he had not experienced in person the difficulties of doing things, the difficulties of artistic creation: 'My mother told me: Whatever you do, do it!'

We have seen on numerous occasions that there was often a marked discrepancy between the statements made by the occupants and their actions. In fact, in a number of cases, these were diametrically opposed to one another. Moreover, we have also seen that there was a discrepancy between Le Corbusier's intentions and his finished works. But although both the occupants and Le Corbusier were less than consistent, in the final analysis they complemented one another extremely well for, by designing open-plan interiors, Le Corbusier provided the occupants with a perfect basis for their conversions.

This consistency of action between architect and occupants seems to have derived in the first instance from the 'construction game' utilized by Le Corbusier in Pessac, which led on quite naturally to the 'conversion game' subsequently played by the occupants. Thus, the rules of the game framed by Le Corbusier proved extremely fertile.

Of course, the whole basis of these games was standardization, for this determined the form and size of the component elements. But both the architect and, subsequently, the occupants were able to play about with these components until they discovered suitable arrangements. This was done by the occupants in terms of their own individual houses and by the architect in terms of the whole district. The geometrical permutations were considerable, which meant that differentiation was assured. In the final analysis my own enquiry has also been concerned with topographical considerations for, after first investigating the ecology of the Q.M.F., I have been able to proceed to a topographical analysis. Gradually, the *situational* factor has emerged more and more clearly and has been defined in terms of open and closed, of external and internal, characteristics. Such antitheses appear primarily within a situational framework; and so, before playing black or white, it is necessary to know how to play on the antithesis between black and white. Consequently, instead of trying to decide whether, in the final analysis, Le Corbusier's architecture is open or closed, I have preferred to concentrate on its antithetical character, which derives from the polarity between external and internal or – and this comes to the same

163

thing in the end – open and closed conditions. This polarity is, of course, one of the fundamental characteristics of urban space and – in so far as it is possible to conceptualize space or, conversely, to spatialize mental concepts – it helps us to effect the transition from urban space – or architecture – to thought. Meanwhile, the question as to whether Le Corbusier's architecture is open or closed must remain unanswered:

s — If I have understood you correctly, there is a kind of architecture which creates enclosed spaces and another kind which creates open spaces or, rather, which is capable of creating open spaces provided – and, again, I hope I have got this right – you have the appropriate means at your disposal . . . But what would you say were the sort of things that have to be done in order to produce a completely open or a completely closed form of architecture?

M — How can we best describe the kind of architecture that produces an enclosed space? Has anyone any suggestions?

B — There are plenty of examples, certainly.

M — Yes, that's true . . . I would say that it encloses both external space and internal space by its solidity, by its firmness (but not in any rigid sense), by its immutability, by a kind of monumental presence; and this applies even to quite small buildings, even to the suburban villa we were talking about a moment ago. That is certainly an example of closed architecture. On the other hand that may well be the very thing that people hanker after; that may well be what they want. Basically, I'm not at all sure they really want to play *Lego*.

As far as open architecture is concerned, that's a bit more difficult. There's camping, of course. But, in the final analysis, I suppose that's a form of closed architecture too.

E — The people who live under bridges enjoy an extremely open style of architecture.

M — That's very true! And nature has also produced open architecture, even more open than under bridges.

a — But what about Pessac? Is that open or closed?

M — I think that Le Corbusier tended to produce closed architecture.

a — Yes, but what about Pessac? It is an example of Le Corbusier's architecture, so can we talk about that? We have all the documents.

M — Trying to visualize what Le Corbusier had in mind forty years ago, it seems to me that he certainly enclosed things to some extent. But then, if we look at the photographs which he has left for us, we also see that this was a man who dreamt his dream, high up on the terraces. I believe that, standing and looking at his work at ground level, he will have recognized its immutability, but he will also have hoped that on the roof gardens people would rediscover open spaces.

Illustrations

At Lège, near Arcachon,
Le Corbusier built ten houses
for Henry Frugès shortly before
undertaking the Pessac project.
They were more or less the
prototype for the villas of the
Q.M.F. and, like them, have been
extensively modified.

1
The houses in Lège have suffered
from a form of rural mimesis that
is even more disfiguring than the
suburban mimesis found in
Pessac.

2
The narrow slit on the extreme
right seems almost futuristic.

3
Occasionally, in odd corners, we
find reminders of Le Corbusier.

4–11
In Lège the original 'roof-terraces' have all
been spanned by pitched roofs. The terraces
have been converted into rooms and the wide
windows have been made narrower.
On the left, original condition, on the right,
present condition (1967).

4

6

8

10

5

7

9

11

Pessac: views of the three roads in the settlement showing the different types of houses built by Le Corbusier from 'identical cells'.

12
Rue Le Corbusier: three-storeyed semi-detached houses. Each house contains the same component cells placed back to back (type 3).

13
Rue Henry Frugès: terraced houses. Every other house faces in the opposite direction (type 1).

15
In this terrace not a single 'wide window' has survived. The outline of the original window is still clearly visible on the second house from the left (type 1).

14
Rue des Arcades (formerly Rue Vrinat):
these otherwise detached houses are linked
by 'arcades' and so form a continuous
terrace. The arcade just visible on the
extreme right has been completely closed
up (type 2).

18–21
The continuity of Le Corbusier's
homogenetic and identical façades has
been disrupted by the creation of separate
and highly individual façades (type 1).

16
A typical 'lean-to' house built opposite the
Quartiers Modernes Frugès in 1930,
i.e. shortly after their completion.

17
The back addition is clearly visible in this
view.

22–23
The storage space provided at
ground level has been converted
into a garage (type 1).

24–25
Here the 'wide windows' have
been reduced in size and the open
area beneath the stilts has been
enclosed (type 3).

26–27
Here too the open area beneath
the stilts has been enclosed
(type 2).

22

24

26

23

25

27

28–33
**Originally these semi-detached houses were
painted in contrasting colours, each pair of
houses being treated as a single unit in this
respect. Today the original polychromy has
disappeared and the semi-detached status
of the dwellings is readily apparent.**

Photograph reproduced from
*Le Corbusier et Pierre Jeanneret,
Œuvre Complete: 1910–1929*
(Zurich, 1965).

28

34

34–35
Apart from adding a cornice the occupants
of this house have not changed the original
façade (type 3).

36
Here we see a façade actually being
converted. The newly rendered sections of
the wall stand out quite clearly.

37–38
The 'see-through' quality of the terraces has completely disappeared as a result of the conversions.

39–41
Here the architectural character of the original building has been completely destroyed by the modification of the apertures, the enclosure of the terrace, the installation of a pitched roof and the introduction of an annexe (type 3).

39–41

37

42–43
Le Corbusier's architecture considered
from the point of view of boat design.

44–47
The arches which link these adjacent houses
provided open areas which have been
exploited in a variety of ways. In some cases
they have been completely blocked off
(type 2).

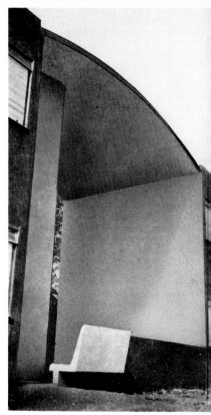

47

44

46

48–54
The open staircase on the front façade of
this detached house was one of Le
Corbusier's most attractive ideas. I was
unable to interview the occupants but the
fact that they have used the landing of the
staircase as a verandah would perhaps
suggest that they were aware of its appeal.
On the other hand, they have enclosed the
area beneath the stilts and blocked off part
of the terrace, although the 'wide windows'
have survived (type 6, detached).

48

46

48–54

The open staircase on the front façade of
this detached house was one of Le
Corbusier's most attractive ideas. I was
unable to interview the occupants but the
fact that they have used the landing of the
staircase as a verandah would perhaps
suggest that they were aware of its appeal.
On the other hand, they have enclosed the
area beneath the stilts and blocked off part
of the terrace, although the 'wide windows'
have survived (type 6, detached).

48

55–59
Decoration:
The decorative features introduced by
the occupants reflect all manner of
different styles but never cubism.

55–59

60–64
Vegetation:
Trees and shrubs also enable the occupants
to express their personalities.

60–64

The difference in appearance between zone A and zone B.

65–67
In this zone the appearance is 'coquette' . . .

65

68

69

6

67

0

68–70
In this zone the appearance is dilapidated
(type 1).